Aurora Maria Riviezzo

essays by

Laura Andreini
François-Luc Giraldeau
Filippo De Pieri
Joseph Giovannini

ON THE ROAD city
New York

ON THE ROAD
Editor of collection
Laura Andreini

editorial project
Forma Edizioni srl, Firenze, Italia
redazione@formaedizioni.it
www.formaedizioni.it

editorial production
Archea Associati

editorial direction
Laura Andreini

authors
Aurora Maria Riviezzo

editorial staff
Maria Giulia Caliri
Livia D'Aliasi
Beatrice Papucci

graphic design
Isabella Peruzzi

translations
Katy Hannan

texts by
Laura Andreini
François-Luc Giraldeau
Filippo De Pieri
Joseph Giovannini

Aurora Maria Riviezzo: pp. 30-93,
96-125, 170-193, 196-209
Lorenzo Giordano: pp. 128-165

Aurora Maria Riviezzo, is an Architect and independent researcher. She works as freelance editor and curator, collaborating with architectural studios and Italian publishing houses.
Her personal research focuses on modern and contemporary architecture, with particular attention to second post-war period. She took part in the residency promoted by La Biennale di Venezia for under-30 architecture historians.

First Edition: November 2019

ISBN 978-88-55210-20-1

Table of contents

Guidebook as tool

On the Road is a collection of contemporary architecture guidebooks whose purpose is to tell about a place, whether a city or larger area, through its architectural works chosen to be visited and experienced directly.

The guidebook has a convenient special jacket that opens into a map marking the location of the architectural works and interesting sites to visit. On the back are miniature images and addresses of the architectural works described in detail within.

The book starts with short essays explaining the city or area's present day and history and outlining possible future scenarios with planned or imminent projects. Each work features a photograph of the whole, an architectural drawing (plan or section), a short description, and facts including architect, type, year of construction, address, website, and how to visit it.

The finest architecture of each city and suggested routes are represented by this collection of not-to-be-missed, "timeless" buildings that uniquely define their settings. General information and useful tips for travelers help them optimize their visits and quickly understand the essence of the place described.

Museums, theatres, restaurants, hotels and a list of top architectural firms working in the city let visitors turn a regular trip into an opportunity for study or work.

Note: The pinpoints outside the maps at the beginning of the itineraries are viewable on the rear of the book jacket.

New York

Laura Andreini*

New York is perhaps the city that attracts more visitors of every kind and from every corner of the world for its exciting contemporary architecture. Visitors to New York are immediately aware of being immersed in a context where architecture plays a leading role, and where the background sometimes steals the scene from what is going on in the city.

Over the years, New York has been the scene of some extraordinary architectural experimentation. This includes technical innovations such as elevators and steel and glass curtain walls; urban planning experiments like New York's unique grid system, the decision to recess certain buildings from the street front, or to create new urban accessibility through the High Line; New York is also famous for its cultural experimentation. More than in any other city, architects are required to measure themselves with all that is modern. Examples of this can be seen in the extensions to the Whitney Museum of American Art and the MoMA. Eclectic designs inspired by an intelligent integration of town planning regulations and architectural talent remain orderly, within the clearly defined orthogonal grid system, where coincidental surprise effects are suddenly generated by certain individual buildings.

Leafing through the On the Road guides, readers have access to an authentic catalog of modern and contemporary architecture. New York is the city where some of the world's greatest architects have been able to experiment and express themselves; it is the city where many starchitects have been asked to illustrate their architectural concepts, and where young professionals come to grips with new approaches, brushing with, and even overtaking the limits of avant-guarde design.

This On the Road guide, is aimed at planning a circuit that might otherwise provoke a kind of Stendhal Syndrome in keen enthusiasts: New York is a place that is part of the iconographic heritage in every one of us, even those who have never been there. To be able to come into close contact and to experience its vibrant three-dimensional nature, awakens emotions that we rarely encounter on other occasions. The visit proposed in this book is divided into 5 itineraries, three of which are in Manhattan alone. It is the district of New York with the greatest number of buildings of architectural interest. The other two itineraries refer to Brooklyn and Queens. The list of 84 highly prestigious projects will help readers and visitors increase their appreciation of contemporary architecture in a city where, more than most places, is deeply rooted, but also in constant evolution.

* Laura Andreini is architect and associate professor at DIDA, University of Florence. Co-founder of Studio Archea where she still works, she is also writer and deputy editor for *area* magazine.

Political / geographical facts

country
United States of America, New York State

language
English

area code
(+1) 212, 718, 917, 347, 646

coordinates
40° 43′ N
74° 00′ W

area
784 sq km

population
8,622,698

density
10,998.34 inhabitants / sq km

time zone
UTC-5

city website
www1.nyc.gov

Administrative districts

1. Manhattan
2. Brooklyn
3. Queens
4. Bronx
5. Staten Island

General information
useful addresses and numbers

INFORMATION OFFICES*

www.nycgo.com

Official NYC Information Center
Macy's Herald Square,151 W 34th St
(between Seventh Avenue and Broadway)
+1 212 494 3827
Mon - Sat / 10 am - 10 pm
Sun / 10 am - 9 pm

EMERGENCY SERVICES

Police, Fire Department, Ambulance 911
Emergency medical services 800 395 3400
NY Police Dept 212 560 2730
Contact center 411

URBAN TRANSPORT**

Bus, Train and Subway (26 lines)
Metrocard passes can be bought in all subway stations, from kiosks and automatic vending machines.
Metrocard passes are also available at authorized sales points and can be bought from the official site on line.
www.mta.info/nyct

Ferry boat - NYC Ferry
The NYC Ferry service connects Manhattan, Brooklyn, Queens and the Bronx with East River, Rockaway, South Brooklyn, Astoria, and Soundview routes; in summer it connects Wall Street/Pier 11 with Governors Island. Tickets can be bought on line and at the ferry wharves.
portal.311.nyc.gov

Taxi
YellowCabNYC: +1 800 609 8731
Book Taxy NY: www.booktaxinewyork.com
NYC Taxi Group Inc: +1 718 253 3501
Taxi Workers Alliance: +1 718 706 9892
West Side Airport Taxi Service: +1 929 200 3004
My Taxi Ride Inc: +1 212 920 7641

Car sharing
Car2go, Enterprise CareShare, Via Transportation, GetAround, Storkdriver

Noleggio biciclette
Bike Rent NYC, NY Bike Rental, Central Park Sightseeing Bike Rentals And Tours, Ride Brooklyn

CONSULATE OF THE PEOPLE'S REPUBLIC OF CHINA
520 12th Ave, New York, NY 10036, United States
+1 212 244 9392 / 212 244 9456

BRITISH CONSULATE
885 2nd Ave, New York, NY 10017, United States
+1 212 745 0200

CANADIAN CONSULATE
466 Lexington Ave 20th floor, New York, NY 10017, United States
+1 212 596 1628

RUSSIAN CONSULATE
9 E 91st St, New York, NY 10128, United States
+1 212 534 3782

ITALIAN CONSULATE
690 Park Ave, New York, NY 10065, United States
+1 212 737 9100

HOW TO PHONE

From a local landline: from inside the city, enter the local city code (e.g.: 212 Manhattan) followed by the phone number. When calling from another US city, first enter (001), followed by the city code, and then the phone number.

From a foreign landline: enter the exit code from the country where you are calling, (001) followed by the international code (1) then the local city code (e.g.: 212) and the phone number.

* As well as the information office at Macy's Herald Square there are others at subway stations open from Monday to Saturday, between 10 am and 10 pm, and on Sundays between 10 am and 9 pm.

** Ticket types:
Single Ride Ticket, Base Pay-Per-Ride, MetroCard "Unlimited" (7 days, 30 days, 7 day Express Bus Plus), JFK AirTrain 30-Day Unlimited Ride MetroCard, JFK Air Train 10-Trip MetroCard, Express Bus.
Ferries: One-way adult NYC Ferry ticket, Bike one way, 30-Day pass, 30-Day pass with bike.

Useful tips

1. Moving around New York might seem hard given the size of the city, but it is quite easy to get your bearings: the grid system is divided into Avenues (north to south) and Streets (east to west); they are almost always numbered in consecutive order.

2. The city has a vast range of accommodation for all tastes. Manhattan is the most fashionable, expensive area, with luxury hotels like the Ritz and Baccarat, but there are lots of middle-priced B&Bs, as well as cheaper hostels like the Jazz Hostel chain with dormitories or shared rooms. Brooklyn is the best area to look for accommodation as it offers top solutions for price and comfort.

3. Public transport is very efficient and you can travel quickly around the city. The best option is the subway and many of the 26 lines run even at night. Taxis are practical and not too expensive. The ferry services are easy and practical for quick travel from Manhattan to Brooklyn or the smaller islands, with 8 routes that cross the East and Hudson Rivers every half hour (only during daytime).

4. Street Food is the most authentic local food in New York. Do not miss the hot dog experience from one of the street carts (average price $3), and Nathan's, that first opened on Coney Island in 1916. Other traditional alternatives are the Green markets, local markets scattered around the 5 boroughs where you can try typical local foods and products. Or try Km 0 (www.grownyc.org). Or try a meal at a steakhouse or a hamburger eatery, open all day long, on almost every street corner.

5. The best panoramic views to be seen in Manhattan are from the classic list: Floor 102 of the **Empire State Building/16**, or The top of the Rock inside the **Rockefeller Center/23**. A view of Manhattan from a distance, as well as from up high is a breathtaking experience: take a walk along Brooklyn Bridge, sit on the wharves in the city park below for fantastic front views of Manhattan. Great panoramic views can be had from transport like the boat trips from Battery Park and the Roosevelt aerial Tramway from Upper East Side.

6. New York is one of the world capitals for art, and the artistic panorama includes all fields of theater, music and art exhibitions. As well as the famous museums like **MoMA/25** or the **Lincoln Center/33**, try to see some of the dynamic experimental theaters that promote emerging actors in every corner of the city: (Chelsea, Soho and Williambsurg). The small Off-Off-Broadway theaters have interesting productions at about $15 a ticket, and there are wonderful free productions of "Shakespeare in the Park" at the Delacorte Theater (limited seats and many requests).

7. Shopping is a fundamental part of travel. For clothing, the big department stores like Century21 and Macy's are good value, or you can hunt out sudden sales that are organized even by designer labels in various areas of the city: there are several sites for this info, updated in real time, such as Sample Sale Records on lazarshopping.com. Others are in the world-famous areas of 5th Avenue, Soho and Nolita; even Brooklyn has become a trendy shopping district for all styles and budgets. During the weekends, many areas hold flea markets and open-air markets, mainly selling retro, vintage, and collectibles. The most famous is the Brooklyn Flea market, with different sales points in Dumbo and Williamsburg districts (www.brooklynflea.com).

8. Carved out of the dense grid system of the city, New York has a large number of well-equipped green spaces and spacious parks. The biggest is Pelham Bay Park in the Bronx, but you can find small green oases among the skyscrapers for a relaxing stroll. As well as iconic **Central Park/41**, we would recommend Prospect Park, opened in Brooklyn in 1866, Bryant Park in Midtown, Washington Square Park at the very center of Greenwich Village, and the small Bowling Green, the oldest in the city, and famous for its Charging Bull, symbolic statue of Wall Street. Coney Island and Brighton Beach are at the southern tip of Brooklyn, and are connected by a boardwalk about 2.7 miles long.

9. The city is rich in events all year long: festivals, parades, religious and national commemorations. The most important are July Fourth, Independence Day, with spectacular fireworks displays on the East River, Halloween and Thanksgiving (November) and Gay Pride (June) parades. At the beginning of October, Open House New York is one of the main events in the field of architecture and design, and includes seminars, conferences, in-house architectural studio visits, and guided tours throughout the city.

10. Ironically, Little Italy is an area truly worth visiting in New York... as is Chinatown: starting from Chatam Square, Bowery and Canal Street you will find the main streets in Chinatown, full of stores, herbalist shops, and street vendors. If you continue towards Little Italy, Mulberry Street flies the red, white and green flag with good Italian cafes and restaurants.

11. A highly recommended visit is a trip to Ellis Island, symbol of the enormous flow of migrants between 1892 and 1954, with an average of 12,000 arrivals per day. One of the 19th century buildings houses the Immigration Museum containing a database that can be consulted to obtain information on personal family. The Ellis Island visit includes a visit to Liberty Island with a 15 minute boat crossing by ferry: departures from Lower Manhattan every 15-30 minutes.

An Historical Primer to New York's Concrete Royalty

François-Luc Giraldeau*

There are few cities, if any, that have managed to capture the collective imagination to the extent that New York City has. Standing alone as a beacon for opportunity, growth, and possibility, New York City is as much a constructed idea as it is a real-life concrete jungle with its own Empire State of Mind. A confluence of environmental, political, social, and economic factors as much as a study in narrative and mythology, mapping its architectural history is almost as Sisyphean a task as inhabiting it.

There are entire libraries of knowledge detailing New York's built history; from its earliest iteration as a Dutch seaport to post-9/11 reactionary design theories, the City continues to occupy not only the collective imagination but that of the critic and scholar as well. It presents itself as a compelling case study, a microcosmic clash of distinctive styles and movements. With each style and expression heavily charged with its own historical and cultural markers, the search to find coherence is much like finding a needle-in-the-haystack.

The quagmire that is New York's architectural history has lent itself to endless theorizing, perhaps most notably Rem Koolhaas' now-seminal *Delirious New York*, in which the architect posits the City as a laboratory of sorts, a "mythical island" that allows for endless experimentation in design thinking. Koolhaas celebrates the City's eclectic palette as the outcome of two seemingly diametric forces: the stark rigidity of the Commissioners' Plan of 1811 – which established the Manhattan street grid – pitted against the march of time, its ongoing changes in demographics, wealth, technologies, ideologies, and culture. The result is an unconscious "Manhattanism," a built environment that has developed out of an ongoing desire to rectify harsh spatial realities with the optimistic pursuits upon which it was founded.

As my architectural studies drew to a close and the prospect of a new chapter loomed ahead, New York had become, quite literally, a delirious dream of my own. I was seduced by the allure of the City, its promise of endless resources and opportunities, its laboratory-like environment ripe for new ideas and discoveries. Only now, after having spent years trying to earn the right to call myself a New Yorker, have I begun to understand the underlying mechanisms behind what is now colloquially referred to as the "New York-induced delirium."

The reality of New York City and its built environment is one that defies definition. Koolhaas' rendering of New York as a laboratory is an apt metaphor, itself a built space that facilitates dialogues between organic processes and manmade designs. The implicit assumption of a laboratory, however, is that the scientist, thinker, scholar, or creator will be furnished with any and all the tools necessary to carry out his or her experiments. While there is no arguing the conduciveness to design with which New York lends itself, the City is much more battlefield than playground.

* François-Luc Giraldeau is a New York-based creative multihyphenate who has left the traditional practice of architecture to further indulge in a variety of academic, editorial, curatorial, and entrepreneurial activities. He has sought to address questions straddling the architecture-art divide and examine architectural representation as a medium for the investigation of architectural spaces.

Take, for instance, the Commissioners' Plan of 1811, a visionary urban planning concept that portended radical shifts in how the City operates and is experienced by its residents and visitors. Fresh from the victory of the Revolutionary War, New York City was made capital of the newly minted nation, and within five years, became the largest city in the United States, a title Manhattan still holds to this day. With increased scrutiny from both local and overseas officials, city planners soon realized the necessity for a unified streetscape. Rather than fully addressing the scope of challenges presented within the physical limitations of the island's geography, however, the commissioners instead relied on earlier surveys of the land, borrowing heavily from a previous profit-driven commission that favored a division of the land into sellable parcels of real estate. The resulting Commissioners' Plan of 1811 thus irrevocably contributed to the City's overarching mythology of optimism whilst further pitting the romantic ideal against its spatial realities.

An almost immediate pushback to the plan of 1811 – and by far its largest alteration – was the creation of Central Park, again both an ideological response (insofar as to bring the City up to contemporary standards of its European counterparts) as well as a reaction to a growing necessity for public spaces, something largely ignored by the financially-motivated spatial grid. The movement was in large part heralded by wealthy landowners and the elite, yet it represents perhaps one of the first means by which New Yorkers have actively participated in shaping the built environment. Even in its earliest forms, the built environment of New York has been conducive to experimentation, yet much like the guiding principle of its creation, its focus on individualism, autonomy, and the emphasis on progress has lent itself to mutable architectural forms that are inherently meant to be bent or broken, sometimes disregarded and oftentimes reestablished in the very process.

More than anything else, the built environment of New York City is defined by this constant battle – an individual quest for survival in a city established not with any regard to an individual's survival but rather to their capability for progress and success. The reactionary push-and-pull of the metropolis and its residents, each on a perpetual march towards the City's promised mythology of success. New York City, perhaps more than any other city in the world, has and continues to be shaped most by the shared behaviors across an intrinsically disparate community of ethnicities, races, social and economic strata and ideologies. At its core is not any sort of shared basis for identity, but rather a common goal – that of survival and progress. And it is this eye towards survival, towards the future, towards achievements, that contributes most to the built history of the City. New York is the result of stubborn, passionate, and relentless individuals, fighting on a daily basis to prosper in an inhospitable and oftentimes unrewarding environment.

Beneath the mesh of the grid

Filippo De Pieri*

With its apparently Cartesian urban structure, for at least two centuries New York has been the result of the tension between various opposing forces that have influenced the spatial layout as much as the architecture (always supposing that in this city one aspect can actually be distinguished from the other). Here, a pronounced propensity towards artifice is combined with a paradoxical desire to return to an uncontaminated environment; the assertion of a principle of spatial order coexists with its deformation and negation; finally, a strong thrust towards innovation is counterbalanced by the long duration of certain morphological aspects. Contrasts of this kind can be found in many contemporary cities, but more than in other places, in New York they have assumed specific, and in some cases, even extreme forms, making the city an amazing laboratory for experimenting with new urban approaches.

* Filippo De Pieri is an associate professor in History of Architecture at Politecnico University in Turin. His work is focused on the history of European, North American, and Asian cities during the 19th and 20th centuries and contemporary age.

Without a doubt, the most spectacular urban invention in New York is the grid system: the layout for the urban expansion of Manhattan adopted in 1811. The checker-board principle was already a feature in many foundation cities of the new continent, but the ambitious plan drawn up and reinterpreted by the "Commissioners" made it one of the most remarkable town planning experiments of the 19th century. The grid was designed as a practical instrument for a layout that would support the city's development based on commerce and free initiative, as well as the spatial symbol of a new urban model. A large part of the history of the city up until today can be described as the history of the modifications applied to the principles of settlement: a sequence of events that were connected less with the impact of the initial design, than with the successive choices that reconfirmed it, in answer to changing conditions. One of the reasons for the grid's success lies in its capacity to be adapted, following the principles of vertical development, or being able to absorb huge constructions like the Rockefeller Center (1930-39) or the large social housing complexes built in the 1940s and 1950s. It is worth noting that New York is not limited to Manhattan, but covers a much greater urban territory, historically characterized by marked poly-centrism and crossed by a number of different urban settlement systems. During the 20th century, a wide range of different management systems was tested in the vast New York region, from the theoretical decentralization of the Regional Plan of New York and its Environs (1928) through to the reconstruction projects from the 1940s to the 1960s based on federal programs for large infrastructure, services and housing projects. This period marked the emerging of New York as a vast American urban modernism worksite, but also as a city where it was becoming evident that this model was facing a crisis: an outcome in which the symbolic contrast between Robert Moses and Jane Jacobs represents a very powerful narrative. New York is also a city that is focused on self-renewal: it is one of those modern cities in which many large transformations seem to pass from some attribution of new significance to landscapes inherited from a more or less recent past. In fact, the history of the city is marked by the periodic reinvention of its architecture: from Andy Warhol's Factory in the sixties to the appearance of the SoHo lofts in the seventies, and the recent "adaptive reuse" experiments like the MoMA PS1 in Queens. Research into gentrification and residential replacement processes has found an outstanding case study in New York, observed through the trajectory of districts like Williamsburg or the rediscovery of the brownstones in Brooklyn as a type of housing able to attract a clientele of new professionals. In fact, it is no coincidence that one of the "new" buildings most often visited in contemporary New York is a small 19th century factory: the Tenement Museum, preserved and opened to the public in 1998 as a museum to tell the history of immigrant tenements and lifestyles; like no other, it is able to tell the story of a city based on the continuous merging of populations and ethnicities.

The environment in which this melting pot developed has been often presented as extremely artificial, a place where the detachment from nature occurred in a far more radical manner than in other western cities. One of the most famous books written on the architecture of the city: *Delirious New York* by Rem Koolhaas (1978), proposed a theory that all of Manhattan can be read like a "collective experiment", a paradigm for a "culture of congestion" which establishes its own specific rules. This image of complete artificiality originated in the long-lasting imaginary of destruction and catastrophe that has always represented a separate chapter in the narrative of the city, from *King Kong* (1933) to *1997: Escape from New York* (1981), through to recent novels like *New York 2140* by Kim Robinson (2017). According to certain observers, rather than a contrast, New York is representative of a process of reinvention able to give life to a "second nature", the result of the hybridization between natural and technological elements. An emblematic example of this concept is Central Park, the project created by Olmsted and Vaux (1857) as a contrast to the geometrical plan of the city, but also as a way to make it possible for the city to continue. They created a landscape with the complete reconstruction of the existing site, but which was designed to represent a form of nature seen as the access key to some of the most authentic American values. Today, the intervention for the recovery of the High Line offers a no less contradictory case in point. It has become the contested global icon of a possible alliance between capitalism and nature within extremely versatile urban reconstruction processes. New York's relationship with natural elements is conditioned by the city's original topographic location that influenced the initial settlements. It has a unique position as an estuary city, and interactive maps, like those created for the Manhattan project (welikia.org) try to reconstruct and depict (at least virtually) the area before the arrival of European colonists, which seems to represent a kind of underlying foundation layer of the city at the present time. Today, as the risk of climate crisis leads us to reflect on multiple scenarios for change, that distant original condition seems to appear almost like a desirable image of the near future.

New York City

Joseph Giovannini*

With 578 miles of waterfront, including 14 miles of beaches, New York City could have become a Club Med had the city not evolved into America's dominant port city. From its founding by the Dutch in 1625 as New Amsterdam, the city lived off a vast, protected harbor that never iced over. Warehouses and then factories occupied streets adjacent to the working waterfront, while residential districts kept their distance, gravitating to the spine of the island, Broadway, an old Indian trail cresting the length of Manhattan. The original Dutch settlements and then the English town at the tip of Lower Manhattan bequeathed to today's city a scrum of village streets. After the transformative Commissioners' Plan of 1811, however, the city north of Houston Street turned into a grid that conquered the length of Manhattan, up to 155th Street. The grid expressed a desire for control and balance, and a distrust of nature, an urban posture perpetuated even today by a plan that largely ignores the water.

* Joseph Giovannini is a New York-based architect and critic who has written on architecture and urban design for the *New York Times, New York Magazine*, the *Los Angeles Herald Examiner* and many other publications. In his writings, he coined the term "Deconstructionism," which subsequently became the word that named the movement he first identified.

Broadway, which slices through the grid at a diagonal, remains the primary geometric exception to a city whose Cartesianism permeates the entire urban texture down to apartment layouts and bathroom tiles. The street itself remains the city's primary site of public space, and the corner, its moment of urban privilege. Parks were large but few – Central Park, the New York Botanical Garden in the Bronx, and Prospect Park in Brooklyn. Rare was the town square that interrupted the grid.

The transportation infrastructure confirmed the prejudice of the grid against the water: subways in Manhattan run primarily north south, serving residential and commercial districts at the island's center, leaving the waterfronts marginal. Manhattan's recent urban history is marked by attempts to turn the urban sock inside out, with developments and neighborhood parks now gravitating toward the water, particularly along the East River. The old, gritty waterfront has been liberated from shipping that has moved primarily to expansive spaces of the New Jersey waterfront that can accommodate today's vast container yards and vessels.

New York's invention of the safety elevator and the glass curtain wall suited a city whose tight confines pushed buildings into the Z dimension: the long, thin island prevented sprawl, sending buildings up, toward the sky. For the first years of the 20th century, Manhattan regularly claimed the world's tallest skyscrapers – the Singer, Metropolitan Life, Woolworth, Chrysler, and Empire State buildings, and finally the World Trade Center. Commerce fertilized the world's first urban asparagus patch, but the city that thrived on capital never actually acquired the architectural character of a capital. With the notable exceptions of Grand Central, the New York Public Library, Lincoln Center and the United Nations Building, New York's buildings were built for the bottom line, and largely remained commercial rather than civic. The business of the city was profit not government.

By the turn of the 20th century, New York was borrowing its architectural styles from Europe, adapting the Beaux Arts style to the skyscraper, as in the Singer Building, and in some cases, Gothic, as in the Woolworth Building. It was not until the 1916 Zoning Resolution that required high-rise structures to step back to allow sun into the canyons below that New York developed a high-rise character of its own. In his electrifying chiaroscuro renderings from the early 1920s, American architect Hugh Ferris depicted buildings as man-made mountains, summits rising from stepped foothills. He poeticized the new building code, inspiring generations of New York buildings that, collectively, recalled mountain ranges. These stepped, aspiring structures became, to a degree, New York's high-rise vernacular.

Other than for these mountainous masses, imported styles continued. Architects adapted France's Art Déco to such masterpieces as the Empire State Building, Rockefeller Center, the Chrysler Building and the Chanin, most located Midtown, and some along 42nd Street. That major cross-town artery eventually became an architectural history lesson in the high-rise, starting on the east with the United Nations Building by Harrison & Abramovitz (with Le Corbusier and Oscar Niemeyer) and the Ford Foundation Building (Kevin Roche), and at the west end, with the terra cotta, Art Déco McGraw Hill Building by Raymond Hood.

Already by the early thirties, Art Déco was challenged as the predominant modernist style. The Museum of Modern Art imported Germany's Bauhaus to New York with the International Style Show of 1932, though the most notable specimens were delayed until after the War, when the most famous were built: the Seagram Building by Mies van der Rohe; Lever House by Gordon Bunshaft of Skidmore, Owings and Merrill; and the CBS building by Eero Saarinen. Frank Lloyd Wright was perhaps the most notable apostate resisting the International style, designing the famously unbuilt St. Mark's Tower, structured organically like a tree, and later the Solomon Guggenheim Museum, which broke the wall of box buildings lining 5th Avenue. Eero Saarinen created the avian TWA Building taking off at what was then Idlewild Airport, and Marcel Breuer built his brooding, Brutalist Whitney Museum of American Art. Whether Bauhaus, Expressionist or Brutalist, these buildings rank among the city's handful of modern post-War masterpieces, surprisingly few given New York's wealth, building energy, and cultural centrality.

Until the 1980s, developers in New York remained remarkably uninterested in hiring modern masters, but after flirting with the suburbs, corporations returned to the city with an architectural vengeance, hiring the likes of Kevin Roche (E. F. Hutton Headquarters), Philip Johnson (550 Madison Avenue), and Edward Larrabee Barnes (the IBM and Equitable towers) to design architectural icons, most with architectural crowns acting as logos branding the sky. Modernists like Roche and Barnes even gave in to Post-Modernism in these efforts. With new lighting technology, their iconic tops established the roof of the city, though because of the scale of the buildings, and the size, function and cost of lobbies, the surrounding streets lost the granular urban detail of the neighborhood buildings they displaced. New York's home-grown urban theorist Jane Jacobs, who did so much to save the grain of the city from freeways, at least in Greenwich Village, was ceding ground to an equal urban threat, corporate anomie. Midtown Manhattan was being Houstonized.

Avant-garde architects were conspicuous by their absence in these large-scale corporate commissions, but by 1999, Richard Meier started a trio of condominiums along the Hudson that set the new precedent of designer towers in Downtown neighborhoods. A generation of affluent New Yorkers decamped from Park and 5th avenues for a downtown lifestyle in loft-like structures. Architects included Neil Denari, Bernard Tschumi, Herzog & de Meuron, Zaha Hadid, OMA, Jean Nouvel, Shigeru Ban, Jeanne Gang, and Frank Gehry, who also designed a commercial equivalent, the IAC Building, with billowing glass facades sailing along the Hudson.

The hugely popular High Line, a linear park built on an abandoned elevated rail line by Diller Scofidio + Renfro and landscape architect James Corner Field Operations, stimulated the market for many of these buildings, accelerating gentrification Downtown. But the designer buildings were the products of the even larger forces of globalization that pooled money in New York. With it came a globalized talent pool.

The financial pressures that found expression in avant-garde buildings for wealthy patrons had started at least forty years earlier as Manhattan attracted an increasingly uniform demography of high-earning New Yorkers whose life-styles might differ, but who reported similar income levels to the Internal Revenue Service. New Yorkers who had previously found financial refuge in neighborhoods like SoHo, NoHo, the Meat Packing District and Hell's Kitchen started migrating to one of New York City's four "outer" boroughs, particularly Brooklyn, where zoning limited heights and where architects designed innovative, even avant-garde buildings that sustained the granular character of their low-rise neighborhoods. The Barclays Center by SHoP Architects, an arena in Brooklyn's Downtown, brought the new, young energy of Brooklyn to a large-scale, computer generated project.

If Meier's Perry Street buildings on the Hudson ushered in a new building type Downtown, Christian de Portzamparc prototyped another Midtown in the same year, 1999. His shard-like LVMH Tower on 57th Street, perhaps the city's first avant-garde commercial high-rise, was arguably the most innovative commercial structure since the Seagram Building. Though Deconstructivist, and very much in the anti-corporate spirit of the avant-garde, his tower recast Hugh Ferris's stepped buildings into a façade of inclined planes, providing another answer to New York's zoning codes. The impact of Portzamparc's design was felt only after 9/11, when building activity resumed after the traumatizing attacks. In 2003, SOM finished the angular, spectral Time Warner Center towers, and later, COOKFOX designed the Expressionist Bank of America Tower on 42nd Street. Both buildings carried forward LVMH's spirit of faceted, angular, crystalline towers and underlying notions of complexity and fragmentation.

In 2019, Kohn Pedersen Fox tested the same idiom at even larger scale with two of New York's most monumental towers. James van Klemperer designed the obelisk-like One Vanderbilt with angled street walls opening views onto Grand Central. Not far away, William Pedersen hyphenated two very tall office towers, 10 and 30 Hudson Yards, with a seven-story retail structure. In a city typified by architecture that for decades had translated the urban grid into Cartesian facades, the KPF structures defiantly broke the box at very large scale with inclined facades and eroded volumes that acknowledged exceptional moments in the surrounding streetscape. The inclined planes simply reflected the practical fact that elevators drop from cores at higher floors. In the case of 10 and 30 Hudson Yards, the leaning, dancing towers seem to stir the surrounding towers, energizing them into a three-dimensional field of motion that engages its colleague in the sky, the Empire State Building, not far away.

In the New York tradition of Hugh Ferris's mountain ranges, the KPF towers are dolomitic in their Alpine drama, with sheer mountain faces, some of them calving. New York has come a long way since the Déco design of Rockefeller Center, which was elegant, surely, but controlled rather than exuberant, and tame rather than wild. In the context of a project larger than Rockefeller Center aimed at the global economy, the towers, ironically, are based in New York codes from which their forms grow. The global call of their mountainous majesty draws on a local tradition and the simple need to bring light through Manhattan's canyons down to the street grid to which New York has been accountable since 1811.

432 Park Avenue
UPPER EAST SIDE
BROOKLYN
Central Park
Solomon R. Guggenheim Museum
UPPER WEST S
Riverside Park

Empire State Building
One World Trade Center
Chrysler Building
HELL'S KITCHEN
Hudson River
© Simon Garcia

Brooklyn Bridge
70 Pine
Bank of America
Financial Center
Empire Fulton Park
Jane's Carousel
Pier 17

One World Trade Center
Gehry Building
Four World Trade Center
St -
Building
The Woolworth Building
Southbridge Towers
IPIC
© Marcio Gianotto / Shutterstock

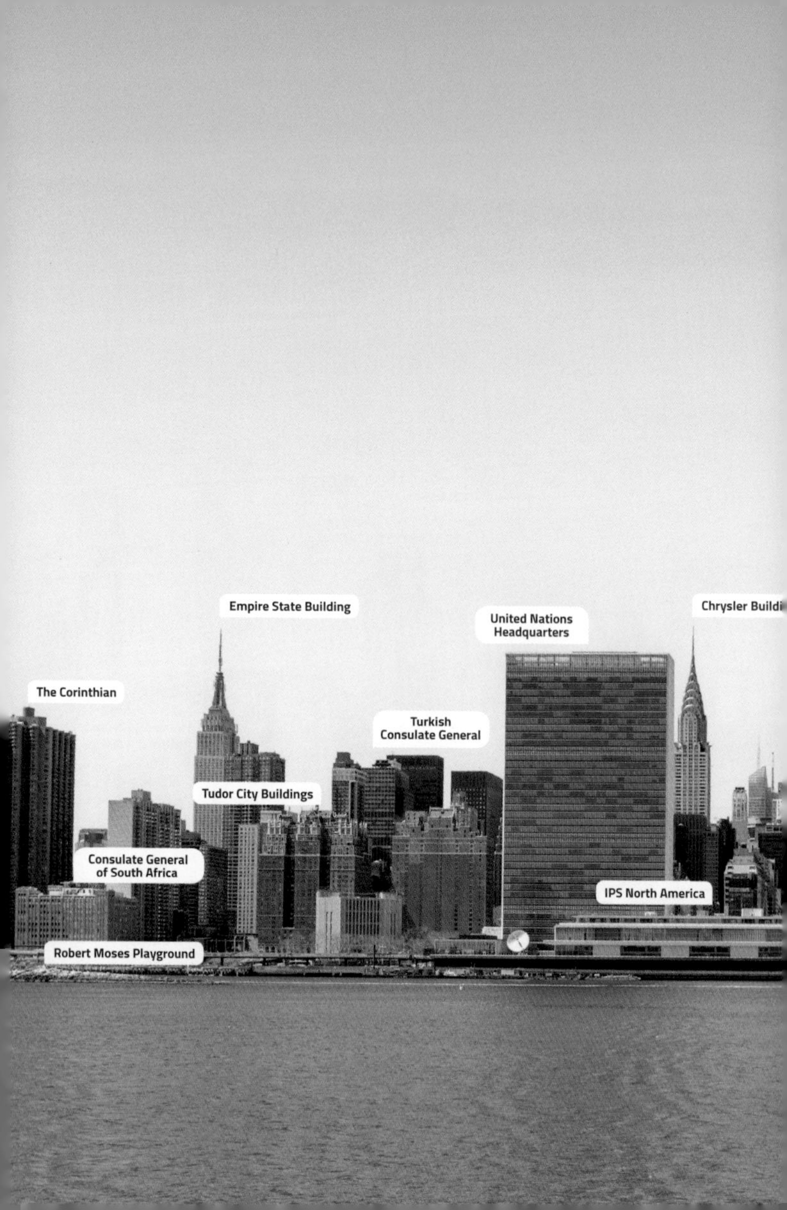

Empire State Building
United Nations Headquarters
Chrysler Buildi
The Corinthian
Turkish Consulate General
Tudor City Buildings
Consulate General of South Africa
IPS North America
Robert Moses Playground

Trump World Tower
50 United Nations Plaza
100 United Nations Plaza
601 Lexington Avenue
UN Apartments
rtle Bay Towers
One Beekman Place
United Nations Visitor Center
UN Gift Garden

Strategies for visiting New York

A visit to New York means diving into its frenetic urban rhythm, and to do the city justice, you should consider at least a week. The projects presented in this book provide a very comprehensive and diverse selection of the city's architectural heritage, with the main focus on contemporary architecture, plus a description of Central Park. The book includes five itineraries, three of which are centered on Manhattan, and the shorter two, that cover Brooklyn and Queens.

Itinerary A / Midtown Manhattan
Times Square/01 is the perfect starting point for visiting New York: the new pedestrian plaza is the hub of New York, attracting an endless flow of tourists; its flashing advertising and billboards symbolize "the city that never sleeps." The first itinerary is the most intensive and includes the entire Midtown district, the nerve centre of the city, with its densely packed skyscrapers. This route includes iconic Art Déco structures like the **Empire State Building/16** and the **Chrysler Building/18**, but also radical design such as the **Ford Foundation/19**, the **Seagram Building/21** and the **Rockefeller Center/23**. A fundamental part of this itinerary is Hell's Kitchen, on the West Side, where you can walk along the overhead urban park, **The High Line/05**, to visit certain recently constructed major projects designed by international architects: **The Shed/07**, the **IAC Building/09** and the **Solar Carve/10**. The route continues down to the lower part of Midtown and includes the area around the **Flatiron Building/11**, then moves back up the other side along East River. The final stage is a return to the north-east end of Murray Hill with the **Mercedes House/31** and **VIΛ 57 West/32**, projects that in different ways, have launched a new style of architecture half-way between the American skyscraper and the European courtyard building.

Itinerary B / Upper Manhattan – Harlem
The second itinerary covers the northern portion of Manhattan as far as Harlem. It follows the geographical division defined by **Central Park/41**, to which we have dedicated a specific map with eleven essential points of interest. The recommended starting point is the **Lincoln Center for Performing Arts/33**, where you can visit individual buildings, including the famous **Julliard School/36**. Continuing on foot along Amsterdam Avenue, you will reach the **American Museum of Natural History/39** and the **Rose Center for Earth & Space/40**, adjacent to the museum and next to the park. On the East Side, the Museum Mile contains some of the most famous galleries and museums in the world in a single stretch along 5th Avenue. Not to be missed is the **Solomon R. Guggenheim Museum/42**. This route closes with three stops that connect the historic campus of Columbia University with the new **Manhattanville Campus/45** and the **Roy and Diana Vagelos Education Center/46**.

Itinerary C / Lower Manhattan
The southern part of Manhattan is the historic heart of the island, and the road system does not correspond with the grid system laid out in 1811. The best way to discover this area is on foot, through Greenwich Village, the Bowery, Soho, Tribeca and Wall Street. This route includes a wide range of architecture, from high fashion boutiques like **Prada Epicenter/53**, to museums, high-rise residential towers, and office blocks. It is concentrated in the area of the World Trade Center, with the **9/11 Memorial/62** created in 2011 and the **Memorial Pavilion/61**. From Battery Park, on the southernmost tip, ferries will take you to Ellis Island, Liberty Island and Governors Island: **The Hills/65**.

Itinerary D / Brooklyn
Brooklyn is by far the most dynamic district in the city; vast redevelopment schemes are underway to redeem post-industrial areas and buildings. The first stop is the **Empire Store/66** and **Domino Park/76**. We recommend the route through the DUMBO quarter ("Down Under the Manhattan Bridge Overpass") that covers the area between the two bridges, followed by the route along East River as far as the **Brooklyn Bridge Park/68** with breathtaking views of Manhattan. From there, take the subway (B and D lines), to visit the **Brooklyn Public Library/69**, and the **Brooklyn Museum/70**, designed before the district became part of Manhattan in 1896 – and the residential area of Crown Heights where the **Children's Museum/72** is located. The itinerary continues as far as the vast post-industrial Brooklyn Navy Yard to visit the **A/D/O/77** creative hub: a low, graffiti-covered, red brick building that embodies the past and future of this historic district.

Itinerary E / Queens
The Queens itinerary is the shortest, although it covers the largest surface area, up to the northern and western boundaries formed by East River. The first stop is Long Island City, that borders Green Point, Brooklyn and is only one subway stop from Manhattan. Many of the old buildings with their traditional red-brick architecture have been reconverted to create some of the most interesting artistic revelations in the city, like the **SculptureCenter/78** and **MoMA PS1/79**. The riverside area has views of the UN building opposite, and has recently undergone redevelopment to create public parks and buildings like the public library of **Hunters Point/80**. All neighborhoods in this district can be reached by subway line 7, but if you decide to walk northwards along Vernon Boulevard, you will discover a fascinating blend of ethnic and architectural styles before reaching the Astoria area and the Foundation created by artist, **Isamu Noguchi/82**. The last stop is **Flushing Meadows Corona Park/83** that occupies a strip in the center of the district.

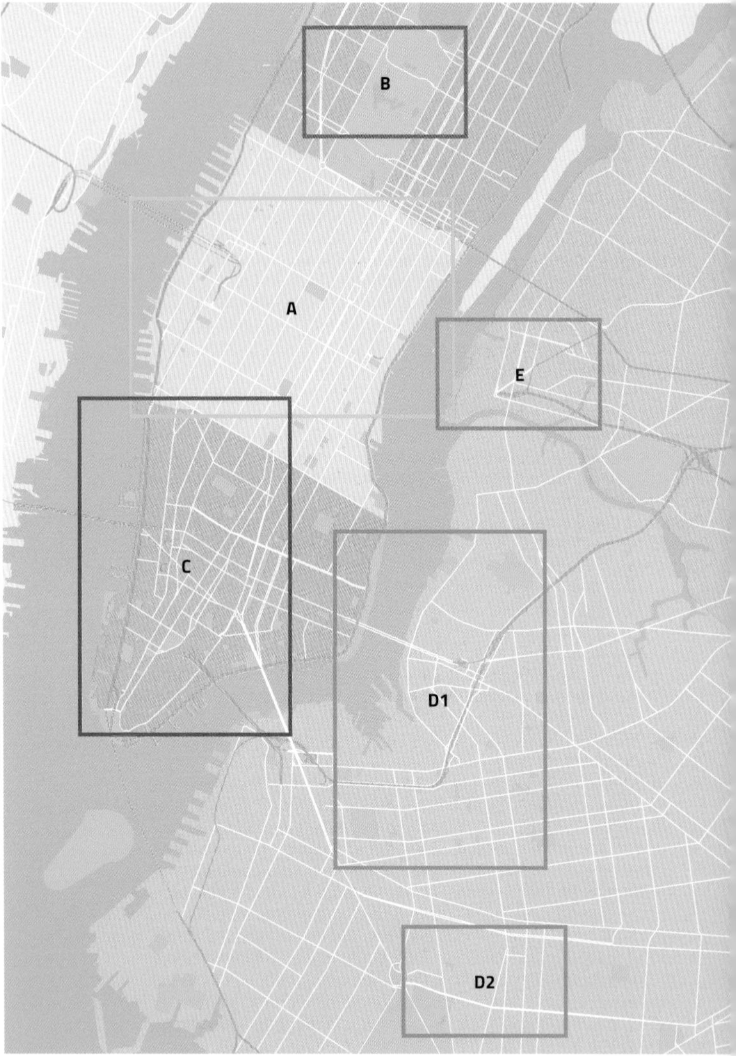
B
A
E
C
D1
D2

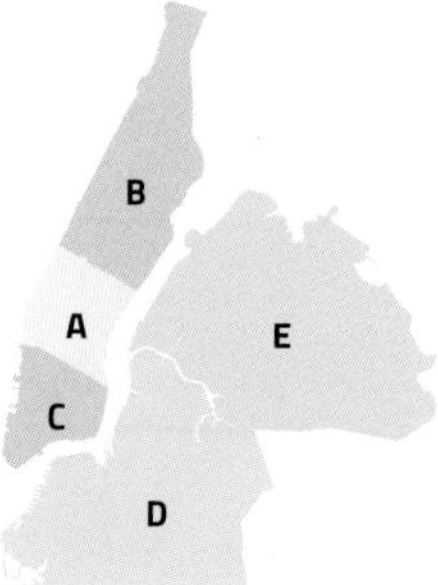

Routes

A. Midtown Manhattan
B. Upper Manhattan – Harlem
C. Lower Manhattan
D. Brooklyn
E. Queens

Midtown Manhattan

01. Times Square
02. Times Square Tower
03. The New York Times Building
04. Javits Center
05. The High Line
06. Vessel
07. The Shed
08. David Zwirner Gallery
09. IAC Building
10. Solar Carve
11. Flatiron Building
12. One Madison
13. 121 E 22nd St
14. Carmel Place
15. Madison Square Garden
16. Empire State Building
17. Morgan Library & Museum
18. Chrysler Building
19. Ford Foundation Building
20. Rockefeller Guest House
21. Seagram Building
22. Lever House
23. Rockefeller Center
24. Radio City Music Hall
25. Museum of Modern Art – MoMA
26. 550 Madison Avenue
27. 432 Park Avenue
28. Louis Vuitton Store
29. Hearst Tower
30. Time Warner Center
31. Mercedes House
32. VIΛ 57 West

0 m
200 m
500 m
New York City Center
The Broadway Theatre
Gershwin Theatre
Circle in the Square Theatre
50 St
50 St B roadway
49 St
Times Square
New Amsterdam Theatre
The Town Hall
42 St - Bryant Park
2 St
Bryant Park
5 Avenue - Bryant Park
Populous
Workshop apd
Empire State Building
Morgan Library & Museum
33 St
St Broadway
18 St
Shake Shack
69th Regiment Armory
The PIT
Gramercy Theatre
57 St
Apple Fifth Avenue
Tiffany & Co.
Trump Tower
Manolo Blahnik
Museum of Modern Art - MoMA
5 Avenue - 53 St station
Radio City Music Hall
Top of the Rock
Rockefeller Center
FAO Schwarz
Grand Central - 42 Street
Lexington Av - 59 St
Bloomingdale's
Tramway Plaza
601 Lexington Avenue
Lexington Av - 53 St
St Bartholomew's Church
Japan Society
Raoul Wallenberg Monument
ONU
The Isaiah Wall
United Nations Headquarters
Robert Moses Playground
Queens Midtown Tunnel (Toll road)
St. Vartan Park
Tisch Hospital
Bellevue South Park
Bellevue Hospital Center
East River
W 51st St
W 50th St
W 47th St
W 48th St
W 46th St
W 44th St
W 39th St
W 37th St
W 35th St
W 32nd St
E 59th St
E 58th St
E 57th St
E 56th St
E 54th St
E 52nd St
E 51st St
E 50th St
E 49th St
E 48th St
E 47th St
E 46th St
E 45th St
E 44th St
E 43rd St
E 42nd St
E 41st St
E 40th St
E 39th St
E 38th St
E 37th St
E 36th St
E 35th St
E 34th St
E 33rd St
E 32nd St
E 31st St
E 30th St
E 29th St
E 28th St
E 27th St
E 26th St
8th Ave
Broadway
6th Ave
5th Ave
Madison Ave
Park Ave
Lexington Ave
3rd Ave
2nd Ave
1st Avenue
Tunnel Exit St
E
F
6
7
8

01. Times Square

Times Square
New York, NY 10036

open to the public

www.timessquarenyc.org

7 / N / Q / R / W >
Times Sq - 42 St

M7 / M20 / M104 >
7 Ave - W 41 St

The iconic landmark, Times Square, is a major crossroads in Midtown Manhattan, and point of intersection between seven high-rise towers and the famous subway station. It is also the core of the Broadway Theater District entertainment business. It is calculated that it is crossed by an average of 333,000 people a day, a figure that was a deciding factor for the decision of the NYC Department of Transportation to radically reconstruct the urban layout behind Times Square. In 2017 the Snøhetta project transformed one of the most congested intersections in the world into a model civic space, carving out 2.5 acres of pedestrian space in the heart of Manhattan. The integrated design solutions have also improved public safety in the area and increased usability because of the strong reduction in noise and air pollution. New uniform paving covers all pedestrian areas. It is composed of a customized blend of prefabricated concrete containing nickel disks that reflect the famous advertising billboards, reinforcing the square's image as a world-wide open-air stage and international icon.

© Michael Grimm

architects
Snøhetta

type
public space

construction
2017

02. Times Square Tower

7 Times Square
New York, NY 10036

external viewing only

+1 212 768 1560
Info@TimesSquareNYC.org
www.timessquarenyc.org

7 / N / Q / R / W >
Times Sq - 42 St

M7 / M20 / M104 >
7 Ave - W 41 St

Times Square Tower is an office tower designed in 2004 by architect, David Childs, president of the New York headquarters of Skidmore, Owings & Merrill for many years. The firm, commonly known as SOM, was founded in Chicago in 1936, and represents the maximum expression of post-war American architecture. Today it is still one of the major architectural firms in the world with more than 10,000 completed projects and 8 international branches. This project is located behind the famous Times building and is the final element in the redevelopment plan for 42nd Street, begun in 2000. The 47-story tower is 726 feet high, and is based on a diagonally reinforced frame structure, clearly visible through the class facade. The internal structural layout is composed of very large flexible spaces that integrate the single office units around the perimeter, and include all services in a central block.

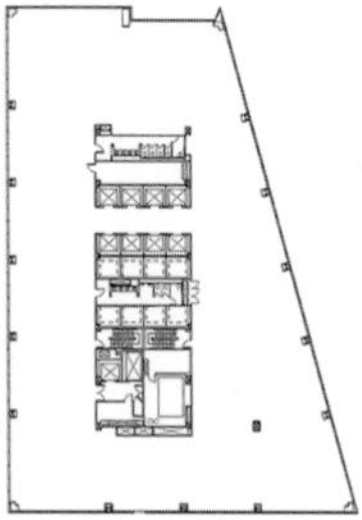

Photo courtesy SOM / © Florian Holzherr

architects
Skidmore, Owings & Merrill

type
offices

construction
2003

03. The New York Times Building

242 W 41st St
New York, NY 10036

open to the public

+1 212 556 4317
TimesCenter@nytimes.com
www.thetimescenter.com

A / C / E > 42 St - Port Authority Bus Terminal
7 / N / Q / R / W > Times Sq - 42 St

M20 > 8 Ave - W 39 St

In 2000, the iconic American daily paper, *The New York Times*, launched an invited competition for the construction of new headquarters as they required more space compared to previous buildings, including the famous Times Tower, which gave its name to nearby Times Square. Among the projects proposed by architects such as Frank Gehry, Norman Foster, César Pelli and Skidmore, Owings & Merrill, the project was assigned to the Italian firm, Renzo Piano Building Workshop. Completed in 2007, the building occupies half a city block with the main facade on 8th Avenue. It is composed of two separate blocks: a low structure set behind a 52-story tower, with a checkerboard layout to reflect the Manhattan grid. A thin, externally visible, steel framework forms the bearing structure of the building. This is clad with a transparent glass wall screened by slender horizontal ceramic rods that act as an energy-efficient sunscreen while flooding the spacious, open interior with natural light. As usual, an essential part of Piano's project is the ground floor, visibly and physically accessible to the public. It houses an auditorium, restaurants, stores and an open-air courtyard garden.

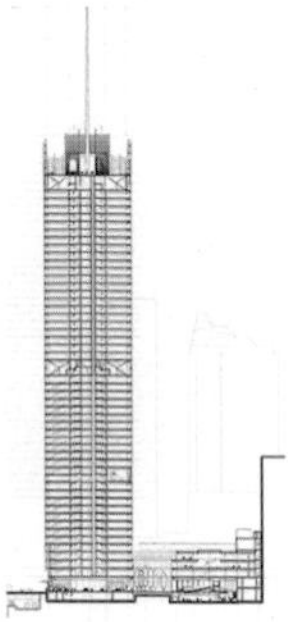

architects
Renzo Piano Building Workshop,
FXFowle Architects, P.C.

type
offices

construction
2007

04. Javits Center

429 11th Ave
New York, NY 10001

Mon - Sun / 9 am - 2 pm

+1 212 216 2000
moreinfo@javitscenter.com
www.javitscenter.com

7 > 34 St - Hudson Yards Subway Station
A / C / E > 34 St - Penn Station

M12 > 11 Ave - W 36 St

The Javits Center is a large trade show and convention center designed by architect James Ingo Freed, partner of the Pei Cobb Freed firm since 1980, together with Ieoh Ming Pei, renowned for the Louvre Pyramid project. The Javits Center is one of the first projects of the redevelopment and conversion plan in West Manhattan along the Hudson River, and is named after senator Jacob K. Javits. The project features a revolutionary structural solution that covers an area of over four city blocks. It is built on a 784,000 square feet rectangular site, and is composed of a modular grid structure based on squares measuring roughly 5 × 5 feet, to guarantee maximum internal flexibility. The building is completely glazed, recalling the Crystal Palace created in London in 1851, with an entrance lobby composed of a series of overlaid glass cubes.
The complex has been modified several times to update the functional and energy features; the space has also been changed by replacing the previous modules with others measuring approximately 5 × 10 feet. In 2013, the American firm Epstein designed and built an extension along 40th Street.

© Pei Cobb Freed & Partners

architects
Pei Cobb Freed & Partners / Epstein, FXCollaborative (extension/renovation)

type
multi-purpose building

construction
1986 / 2013

05. The High Line

Gansevoort St, Washington St
New York, 10014

Mon - Sun / 7 am - 7 pm

+1 212 500 6035
info@thehighline.org
www.thehighline.org

A / C / E / L >
14 Street Station

The High Line is a 1.5 mile-long public park built on an elevated railroad, abandoned since the 1980s, stretching from the Meatpacking District to the Hudson Rail Yards. The project was realized in three different stages and immediately became an international model for the transformation of post-industrial infrastructures and large abandoned urban areas. The park is a wonderful mix of bio-diversity where large numbers of biotypic species alternate with a variety of trees, wild grasses, flowers and colors according to the season. The high Line is exclusively pedestrian and is divided into sections, some paved, others planted, designed according to the heterogeneous urban environments.
The paving is composed of pre-cast reinforced concrete elements laid with open joints that comb into the planted areas, and in some sections, are furnished with seating benches. Ten access points are arranged along the route, and represent a threshold, separating the frenzy of the city from the walkway, a place to stroll, observe and relax.

architects
James Corner Field Operations, Diller Scofidio + Renfro, Piet Oudolf

type
park

construction
2009 / 2011 / 2014 / 2019 - ongoing

06. Vessel

20 Hudson Yards
New York, NY 10001

Mon - Sun / 10 am - 9 pm

+1 646 954 3100

7 > 34th St - Hudson Yards Subway Station

M11 > 10 Av - W 34 St
M34 > 11 Av - W 34 St

Vessel is a symbolic and planimetric hub in the vast Hudson Yards urban redevelopment project, defined as "an urban scale landmark to climb and explore" by its British designer, Thomas Heatherwick. It is a centrepiece that strives to reinterpret the archetype of the staircase as an element of aggregation, taking inspiration from the Piazza di Spagna in Rome and the ancient step-wells in India. It is composed of a self supporting honeycomb structure built from large pre-cast hexagonal modules. It expands as it rises, 150 feet high and the same in diameter, with 154 staircases that intersect at various levels forming 80 landings with panoramic views of the city. Every element, from joins to handrails, was specifically manufactured and individually assembled on site.

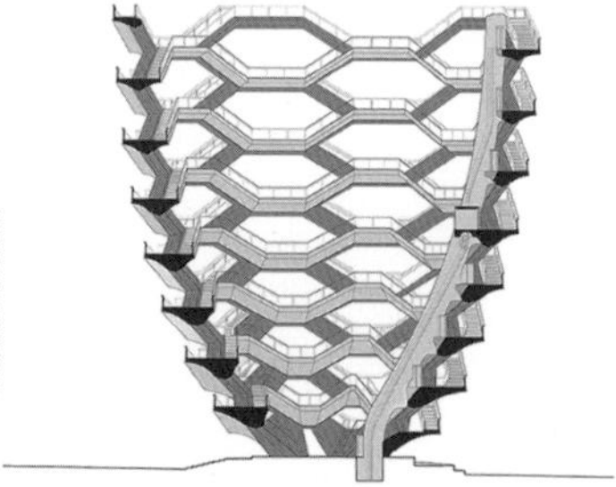

© Heatherwick Studio

© Courtesy of Michael Moran for Related-Oxford

architects
Heatherwick Studio

type
viewpoint

construction
2019

07. The Shed

545 W 30th St
New York, NY 10001

Tue - Sun / 11 am - 6 pm

+1 646 455 3494
info@theshed.org
www.theshed.org

7 > 34th St - Hudson Yards Subway Station

M11 > 10 Ave - W 30 St
M12 > 11 Ave - W 29 St

Among the numerous projects created next to The High Line, The Shed, by Diller Scofidio + Renfro in collaboration with Rockwell Group, is surely one of the most interesting. It is a multi-use, brand-free cultural center, and a creative experimental workshop for visual and performing arts. It is composed of a highly flexible configuration with a range of variations, openings and partitions, able to double its volume with a retractable movable shell that runs on double-wheel tracks, and in only 5 minutes, can extend over the adjacent plaza. This is a form of architecture that does not dictate its use, but can be transformed according to the changing needs of New Yorkers today, and in the future. It is the definition of an innovative architectural practice that can change space and function in continuation, that was inspired by the avant-garde style of the sixties, and more specifically, by projects like Fun Palace by Cedric Price in 1961.

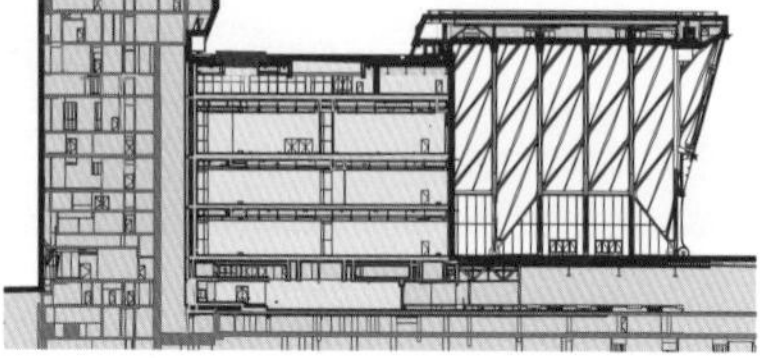

© Iwan Baan

architects
Diller Scofidio + Renfro,
Rockwell Group

type
cultural centre

construction
2019

08. David Zwirner Gallery

537 W 20th St
New York, NY 10011

Tue - Sat / 10 am - 6 pm

+1 212 517 8677
newyork@davidzwirner.com
www.davidzwirner.com

1 / 2 > 23 St Station
A / C / E > 23 St

M12 > 11 Ave - W 18 St
M11 > 10 Ave - W 19 St

In West Chelsea, an exposed concrete building, designed by Selldorf Architects, is home to one of the three New York David Zwirner galleries. It is a project that brings a new identity in its present-day role as a contemporary art incubator, while still resonating with the former industrial history of the neighborhood.
Refined teak is used to frame the rectangular windows and clad the storefront walls in warm contrast with the dark gray concrete facade. A sliding wall in the same wood interrupts the facade at street level to create internal space that opens up towards the exterior. In the lobby, an elegant concrete staircase lit by the overhead skylight connects the five floors of exhibition and office spaces, library and archives. The project also includes five green roof spaces designed by landscape architect, Piet Oudolf, plus premium energy efficiency technology that has earned the project Gold level international LEED certification.

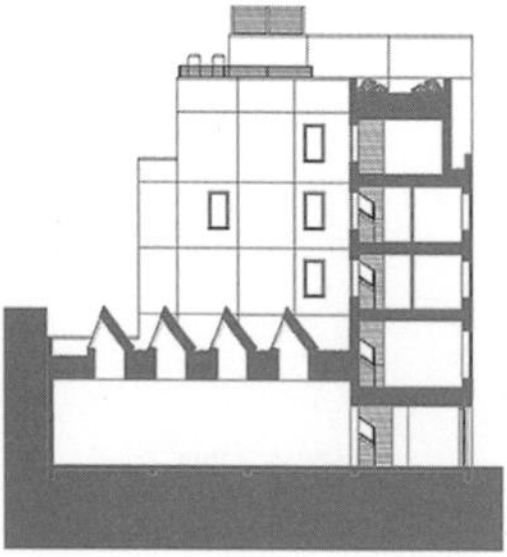

© Selldorf Architects

© Jason Schmidt. Courtesy of Selldorf Architects

architects
Selldorf Architects

type
art gallery

construction
2013

09. IAC Building

555 W 18th St
New York, NY 10011

external viewing only

www.iachq.com

A / C / E / L >
14 Street Station

M12 > 11 Av - W 18 St

The InterActiveCorp headquarters was the first building constructed in New York by the Canadian architect, Frank Gehry, renowned for his strong aesthetic design. The IAC Building is composed of a graceful sinuous structure in sharp contrast with the red brick industrial buildings in the neighborhood, which immediately made it one of the new icons in Chelsea after construction. This ten-story building is composed of two major horizontal blocks, separated by a large terrace area with views of the Hudson; each block is divided into vertical modules in a twisted tower configuration, more strongly accentuated in the upper section, providing a morphological structure that creates a different layout on every floor, with diversified facades on every level. The concrete frame is enclosed in a continuous glass shell composed of 1,150 panels curved on site and supported by fine iron mesh. The full-height windows fade from clear to white, where an opaque ceramic coating is applied to the top and bottom edges of each story.

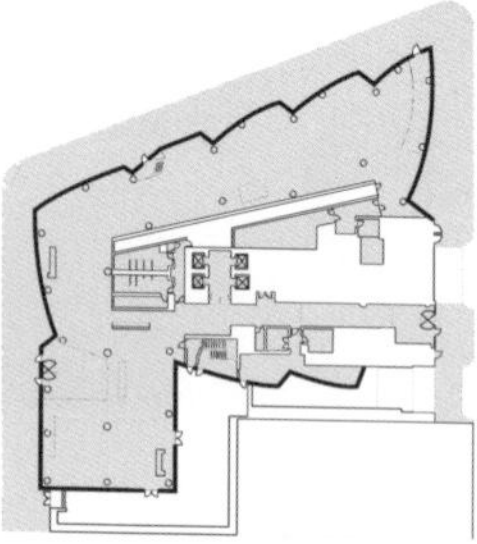

© Brian Logan Photography / Shutterstock.com

architects
Gehry Partners LLP

type
offices

construction
2007

10. Solar Carve

40 10th Ave
New York, NY 10014

external viewing only

+1 646 833 0289

A / C / E / L > 14 St Station

M11 / M12 > W 14 St - 10 Ave

Solar Carve is a commercial tower located on a city site near the banks of the Hudson River and adjacent to the elevated High Line park. The tower is a site-specific project, part of the Studio Gang method aimed at redefining the relationship between vertical high-rise buildings and horizontal planes in city centers, rethinking zoning regulations established for the area in order to create the best conditions for the public realm. By using solar analysis to shape the building according to the incident angles of the sun's path and the consequential shade at the level of the High Line, the architects were able to calculate the geometry of the building to maximize sunlight, fresh air, and river views for people using the park. A podium base covers the whole plot and a large green planted terrace for private use visually joins the High Line level. At the opposite end, toward the Hudson River, the twelve-story tower has a three-dimensional, diamond-shaped, faceted curtain wall that reflects natural light downward into the workspaces and, at the same time, limits the sun's rays from penetrating the interior to improve environmental performance.

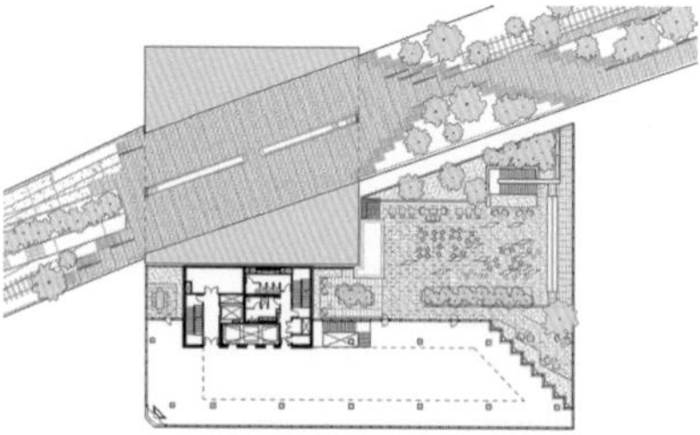

© Studio Gang

architects
Studio Gang

type
offices, retail

construction
2019

11. Flatiron Building

175 5th Ave
New York, NY 10010

external viewing only

N / R / F / M / 6 > 23rd St

M1 / M2 / M3 > 5 Ave - W 20 St

The Flatiron Building was one of the first high-rise buildings created with a futuristic steel frame structure. It was designed in 1902 by Daniel Hudson Burnham, architect and urban planner, one of the leading exponents of the Chicago School. The building takes its name from the shape of the early 20th century cast-iron clothing iron; the iconic architectural structure was dictated by the narrow triangular site that remained after the Manhattan grid pattern had been sliced by Broadway at the height of 5th Avenue. It is built in Beaux Arts style, with a Neo-Renaissance influence, reaching a height of almost 295 feet and measuring only 6.5 feet at its narrowest point. The facades are clad in limestone and enameled terracotta, in a decorative triple structure based on the Greek column, with a base fascia, a shaft with small perforated decorations, and a capital or crowning element composed of arches and columns.

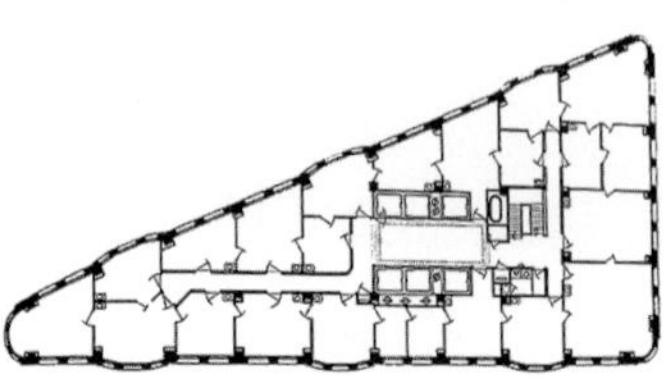

architects
Daniel Hudson Burnham

type
offices, residential

construction
1902

12. One Madison

20 E 23rd St
New York, NY 10010

external viewing only

+1 212 529 5688

www.onemadisonnyc.com

N / Q / R / W / 6 >
23 St Station

BxM7 > E 23 St - Madison Ave

The One Madison residential complex is the most famous project designed by CetraRuddy, founded in New York in 1987 by John Cetra and Nancy J. Ruddy, which today employs a staff of 100 architects and designers.

The complex is divided into three distinct blocks, different in form and function, and located on opposite sides of the site. The main entrance building on 22nd Street, features vertical elements in enameled terracotta. The second square structure houses retail space and common amenities reserved for residents. The tall residential tower is one of the most slender skyscrapers in the city, and towers over the Flatiron skyline at 623 feet with a 12:1 height/base ratio. The main tower shaft bears a series of cantilevered cube pods on the eastern side; each pod is composed of four to six floors and is clad in transparent glass, deconstructing the mass of the building and providing a variety of different apartment types and sizes.

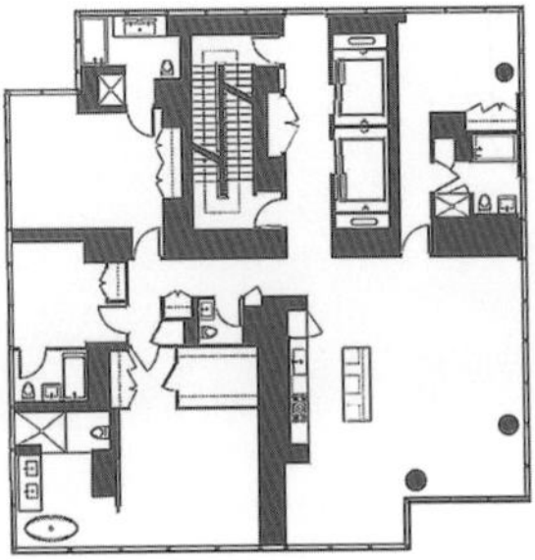

© CetraRuddy

architects
CetraRuddy

type
residential

construction
2010

13. 121 E 22nd St

121 E 22nd St
New York, NY 10010

external viewing only

+1 212 300 4226

www.121e22nd.com

4 / 6 > 23 St Station

SIM6 / SIM11 > E 23 St - Lexington Ave

121 East 22nd Street is the first residential skyscraper designed by OMA in New York under the direction of Shohei Shigematsu, who has been a partner in the firm since 2008. The external design and internal layout were organized in line with the characteristics of the adjacent urban neighborhoods at the intersection of busy Madison Square and the residential Gramercy Park area. The complex is divided into two tower blocks positioned on opposite sides of the same site, connected by an internal courtyard and by the ground floor level that contains shared condominium amenities. The larger building is L-shaped with facades on 23rd Street and Lexington Avenue. It has a uniform facade divided by a regular black concrete grid pattern that is interrupted at the corner by three-dimensional projecting and recessed panels. The formal design of the building is connected and repeated in the facade of the second lower building.

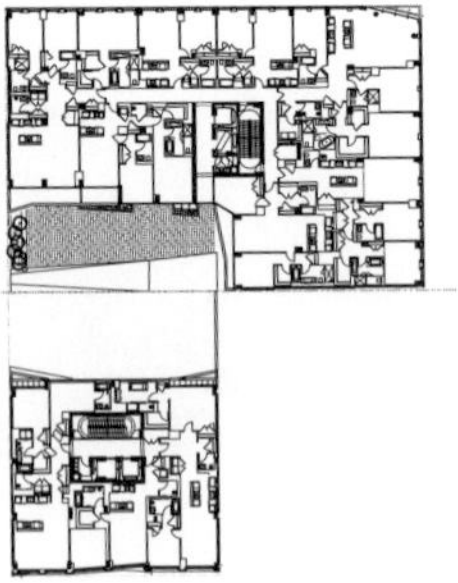

© OMA

architects
OMA

type
residential

construction
2019

14. Carmel Place

335 E 27th St
New York, NY 10016

external viewing only

+1 212 213 3533
info@carmel-place.com
www.carmel-place.com

4 / 6 > 23 St Station

nyc-ferry: AS, LE, SV; Seastreak > E 34th St

M9 / M15 > 1 Ave - E 27 St

Carmel Place is a residential complex constructed as a result of the "adAPT NY" initiative, launched in 2012 by the city Administration's New Housing Marketplace Plan for innovative ideas in urban development. The winning project, designed by the New York firm, nARCHITECTS, represents a modular habitable prototype that is easy to build, expand, or remove, according to necessity. The residential units are built by stacking modules, built and assembled off-site, constructed with a steel frame and pre-cast concrete slab, using a rapid, low-cost, construction process. Carmel Place is currently composed of 55 apartments over nine floors, in eight different sizes and layouts ranging in area from 260-360 square feet. Transported by night, the modules are easily placed in position according to an established configuration. Shared community amenities are located on every floor including the rooftop, and on the ground floor, there is a gym, storage area, and a community meeting room for residents. One of the perimeter modules is designed to contain the staircases.

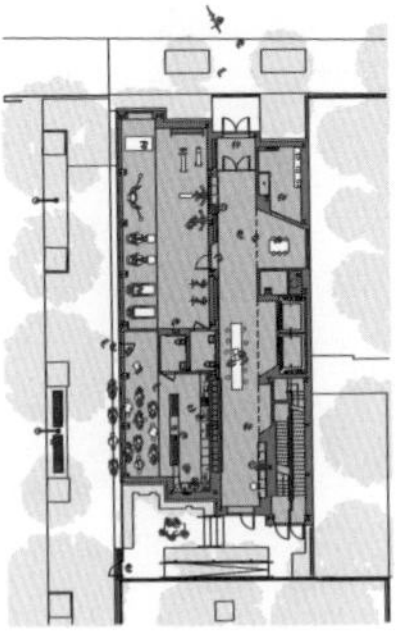

© nARCHITECTS

architects
nARCHITECTS

type
residential

construction
2016

15. Madison Square Garden

4 Pennsylvania Plaza
New York, NY 10001

Mon - Sun / 12.15 am - 3 pm

+1 212 465 6741

www.msg.com

1 / 2 / 3 / A / C / E > 34 St - Penn Station

M7 / M20 > 7 Ave - W 31 St

The first Madison Square Garden arena was built in the late 19th century as an open-air sports stadium next to the Madison Square Park; it was built in 1878 in a Moorish style on a small plot adjacent to the park. The current arena was built on the location of the former Penn Station. The above ground structure of the station was demolished to leave room for the new stadium, provoking such public uproar that it led to the creation of the first New York City Landmarks Preservation Commission. The Madison Square Garden is built in an oval shape and is constructed on 5 levels, plus two underground levels for subway access. The main arena can seat 22,000 spectators. Known as the Mecca of Basketball , it is the official headquarters of the NBA New York Knicks team, but also that of the Hockey League New York Rangers. As well as being famous for boxing and ice skating events it also hosts some of the major musical concerts from around the world.

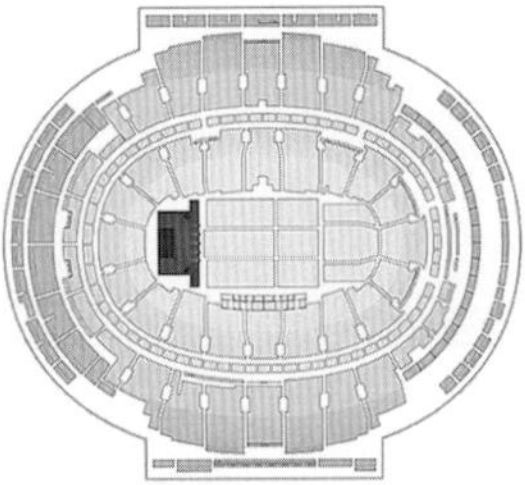

© valeriy eydlin / Shutterstock.com

architects
Charles Luckman Associates / Ellerbe Becket (restoration)

type
sport complex

construction
1968 / 1991

16. Empire State Building

5th Ave W 33rd St
New York, NY 10001

Mon - Sun / 8 am - 2 am

www.esbnyc.com

B / D / N / Q / R > 34 St - Herald Sq Subway Station
1 / 2 / 3 > 34 St - Penn Station

BxM18 > 5 Ave - W 34 St

The Empire State Building is one of America's major landmarks. Built in only 13 months during the Great Depression, it is considered the architectural expression of the American Dream, and is still the most famous and recognizable silhouette on the New York skyline. It is built in the graduated step formation common to high-rise, Art Déco buildings in the 1930s, created by stacking parallelepiped modules on a rectangular base. The building tapers towards the top and is terminated with a pinnacle designed, but never used, to tether zeppelin airships.
The Empire State has a very strong steel structure built on 210 foundation columns sunk into the sturdy granite bedrock of Manhattan, and reaches a height of 1250 feet, with a spectacular panoramic terrace on the 102nd floor. The regular vertical band design gives the building symmetrical impact, emphasizing the soaring effect with limestone cladding alternating with the aluminum strips that surround the windows and terminating with a shell motif. The entrance lobby on 5th Avenue is richly decorated with elegant marble facing and relief detailing in aluminum and gold foil.

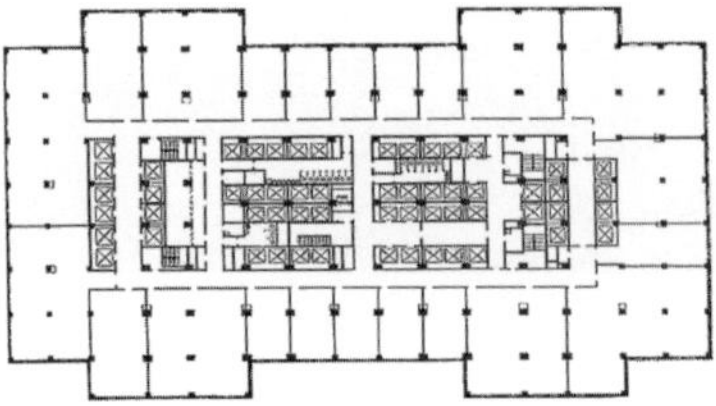

architects
Shreve, Lamb & Harmon

type
offices, museum, viewpoint

construction
1931

17. Morgan Library & Museum

225 Madison Ave
New York, NY 10016

Tue - Thu / 10.30 am - 5 pm
Fri / 10.30 am - 9 pm
Sat / 10 am - 6 pm
Sun / 11 am - 6 pm

+1 212 685 0008

www.themorgan.org

4 / 6 > 33 St Station
4 / 5 / 6 / 7 / S > Grand Central - 42 St Station

M6 / M9 > Madison Ave - E 36 St

The Morgan Library was built in 1906 as the private library of financial magnate John Pierpont Morgan, and housed in an Italianate Neo-Renaissance style building alongside his 19th century residence. It was made a public institution in 1928. The building by McKim, Mead & White was extended and modified over the years until it became one of the most important museums in the city. It is home to the precious Morgan family collection, mainly composed of very rare manuscripts, musical scores, and drawings from every period and geographical origin: for example, early sonatas by Mozart are on show alongside Bob Dylan's jottings for *Blowin' in the Wind*. An important expansion and renovation project was completed in 2006; it was designed by Renzo Piano Building Workshop who integrated the three original core buildings into a single complex, doubling the exhibition space. The new steel and glass additions are inserted between the original buildings and provide a new entrance atrium on Madison Avenue. The structure forms a light-filled plaza for the public in the center of the complex. This extension is mainly constructed with below grade floors, 55 feet deep, and includes a new concert auditorium, the Gilder Lehrman Hall.

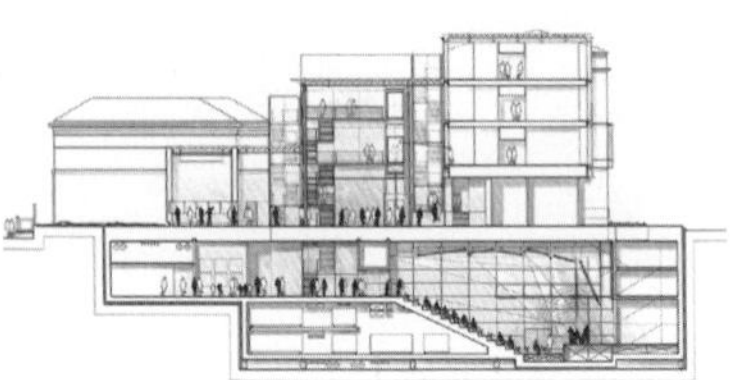
© RPBW

architects
McKim, Mead & White / Benjamin Wistar Morris / Renzo Piano Building Workshop, Beyer Blinder Belle

type
museum, library, bookshop

construction
1906 / 1928 / 2006

18. Chrysler Building

405 Lexington Ave
New York, NY 10174

Mon - Fri / 8 am - 6 pm

+1 212 308 0700 / +1 646 277 9254

www.chryslerbuilding.com

4 / 5 / 6 / 7 / S > Grand Central - 42 St Station

M42 > 42 St - Lexington Ave

The Chrysler Building is an Art Déco masterpiece designed by the New York architect, William Van Alen; it is emblematic of the history of Manhattan and of skyscraper culture in general. It was one of the first buildings constructed in Midtown following the construction and financial boom in the early 20th century, and for a few months, held the record as the world's tallest building, at a height of 1048 feet.
It is composed of a steel load-bearing structure in a regularly decreasing step formation that terminates with the iconic metal spire with its radiating metal arches and triangular windows. The choice of materials and rich internal and external decoration reflect the refined taste applied to Chrysler cars and American cars in general at that time. The corners of the building on the 31st floor are decorated with carved moldings based on the hood ornaments of the early Plymouth automobiles, and the 61st floor corners feature the large Chrysler logo eagle gargoyles. The triangular lobby on the ground floor is faced in red granite and travertine stone. The ceiling murals by the American artist, Edward Trumbull, describe the constructive history of the building, celebrating human endeavor.

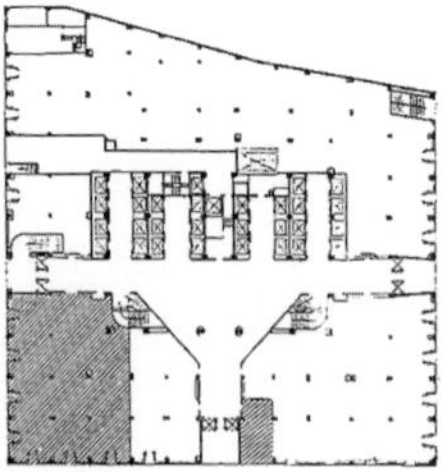

architects
William Van Alen

type
offices

construction
1930

19. Ford Foundation Building

320 E 43rd St
New York, NY 10017

Mon - Fri / 8 am - 6 pm

+1 212 573 5000

www.fordfound.org

4 / 5 / 6 / 7 / S >
Grand Central - 42 St Station

M42 > 42 St - 2 Ave

Designed by architects Kevin Roche and John Dinkeloo in 1967, the Ford Foundation headquarters still remains a strongly innovative project for its urban and structural characteristics, and for the spacious room in the workspace. It is composed of a large square box, 12 stories high, built on a concrete frame with pink granite cladding and Corten steel mesh to support the tall glazed walls. The full height atrium contains an indoor tropical garden designed by Dan Kiley, surrounded on two adjacent sides by offices as far as the last two floors. The office spaces on the top floors run around the whole perimeter. The staggered height sections and stepped back lower floors create terraces at various heights with abundant natural light that filters through the glazed walls and vast skylight. Inside, the very large open space is divided into individual offices of different sizes.
In 2018, the Gensler firm carried out technological and service upgrades throughout the building, and optimized the internal office space configuration, modifying the use of the atrium and the tree species planted there.

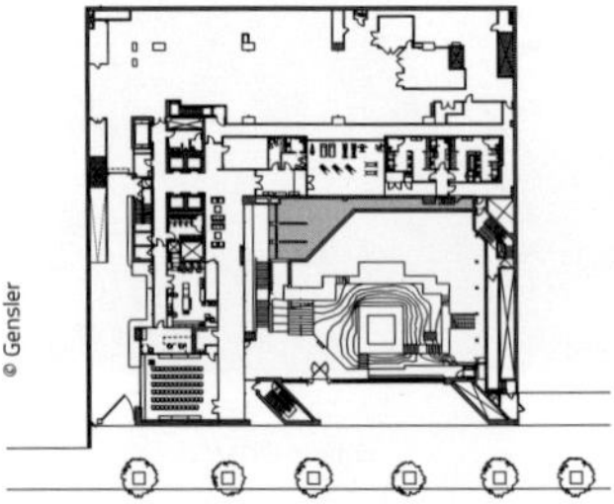

© Gensler

architects
Kevin Roche John Dinkeloo and Associates / Gensler

type
multi-purpose building

construction
1968 / 2018

20. Rockefeller Guest House

242 E 52nd St
New York, NY 10022

external viewing only

M / E > Lexington Ave - 53 St

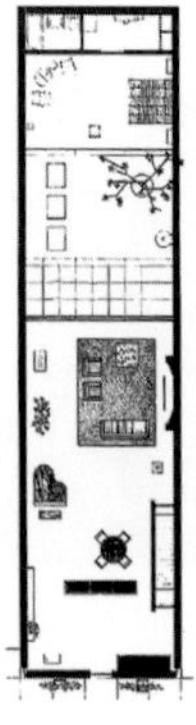

The small house designed by Philip Johnson for Blanchette Rockefeller in 1950 is among the first projects that show the influence of Mies van der Rohe in America, as well as the fundamental elements of International Style, to which Johnson dedicated and curated an exhibition at MoMA in 1936. This project is an alternative interpretation of Johnson's iconic Glass House, built in 1949, both for the long rectangular layout and division of space, and for the choice of materials. It is an elegant structure that occupies a long site measuring 25 x 98 feet between two high buildings. The symmetrical profile reflects the internal layout, with a second floor that is limited to the space above the living room, simply to provide correct height for the street facade. The internal space is divided by an internal patio that separates the large living room/art gallery from the bedroom area, screened by his famous white curtains. Donated in 1958 to MoMA, of which Blanchette was president, the house was sold shortly after and rented in 1971 by Johnson himself, who lived in it for eight years. It was then sold to an anonymous buyer in 2000, for a record sum.

architects
Philip Johnson

type
private residence

construction
1950

21. Seagram Building

375 Park Ave
New York, NY 10152

external viewing only

+1 212 751 5480

www.375parkavenue.com

E > Lexington Av - 53 St
4 / 6 > 51 St station

SIM6 / SIM11 / SIM22 / SIM 26 > Lexington Ave - E 52 St

In 1937, Mies van der Rohe emigrated to USA from Germany for political reasons. He set up an office in Chicago and was director of the Architecture Department of the Illinois Institute of Technology, marking the beginnings of a new American architectural movement, regarded as the Second Chicago School.
After the mid-thirties, the later stage of van der Rohe's career was directed at searching for a strict use of construction techniques combined with monumental architectural form. He achieved this aim with the Seagram Building. It is a slender, single-block, 38-story building, also symmetrical in layout, that manages to express transparency and lightness while being strong and solid. He disrupted the compact street facades along Park Avenue by setting the building back by a third of the site depth to create a public plaza in travertine (a distance that was not in line with development practice that demanded a revision of the City Building Code). The steel framework is hidden behind the curtain wall with an external grid of bronze toned I-beams framing the tinted windows.

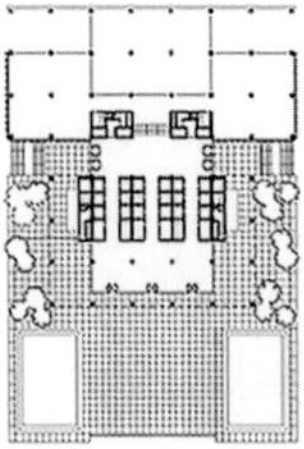

architects
Ludwig Mies van der Rohe,
Philip Johnson

type
offices

construction
1958

22. Lever House

390 Park Ave
New York, NY 10022

Mon - Fri / 8 am - 6 pm

E > 5 Ave - 53 St station

M1 / M2 / M3 > Madison Ave - E 53 St

Lever House, designed by Gordon Bunshaft of Skidmore, Owings & Merrill, was one of the first glass-walled skyscrapers, and marked the turning point in American architecture towards International Style buildings. Breaking with the traditional continuous vertical block model, the Lever House is composed of two contrasting volumes: a harmonious silhouette of 300 feet rises up behind a horizontal building that occupies the entirety of the urban block. The skyscraper is composed of a steel mesh structure that contrasts with the shimmering blue-green glass, interrupted at the end by opaque glass that conceals the service areas. The two-story horizontal building is raised on columns and contains an open public plaza in the center, inspired by Mies van der Rohe and the second Chicago School, and more specifically, by the nearby Seagram Building. The original project envisaged a sculpture garden by Isamu Noguchi within the courtyard, which was only partly constructed when the building was restored in 1998.

© Skidmore, Owings & Merrill

architects
Skidmore, Owings & Merrill

type
offices

construction
1952, 2001 (facade renovation)

23. Rockefeller Center

Rockefeller Plaza
New York, NY 10111

open to the public

+1 212 332 6868

www.rockefellercenter.com

B / D / F > 50 St - Rockefeller Center station
E > 5 Ave - 53 St station

M50 > W 49 St - 5 Ave
M1 / M4 / Q32 > 5 Ave - W 49 St

The Rockefeller Center is a multi-use complex created by John D. Rockefeller during the Depression years. It is composed of 19 buildings designed by different architects, and covers three full city blocks, with a total surface of 22 acres. The complex is an emblematic example in the history of Manhattan because it was conceived as an autonomous functional core: "a city within the city"; it has a layout that also spreads horizontally with underground layers of pedestrian and vehicle routes, a vast retail center, and the subway. The heart of the site is the Lower Plaza, dominated by the 850 foot Comcast Building, (ex-RCA building), the highest structure in the complex. The Plaza and tower were designed by Raymond Hood. The first buildings were designed in Art Déco style, enhanced with sculpture, paintings and mosaics depicting the theme: "The Progress of Man, his achievements through the centuries in art, science, and industry". The four skyscrapers on the west side were built later in the 1960s in International Style.

architects
Reinhard and Hofmeister, Harvey Wiley Corbett, Wallace K. Harrison, Raymond Hood

type
multi-purpose complex

construction
1939

24. Radio City Music Hall

1260 6th Ave
New York, NY 10020

Mon - Sun / 9.30 am - 5 pm

+1 212 465 6000

www.msg.com

B / D / F > 50 St - Rockefeller Center Station
1 > 50th St - Broadway

QM1 / QM2 / QM3 / QM4 > 6 Ave - W 48 St

The Radio City Music Hall was the first building constructed in the Rockefeller Center and owes its name to Rockefeller and David Sarnoff, president of the Radio Corporation of America and the theater's first tenant. A competition was held to decide the interior design, and was won by then unknown Donald Deskey, with an Art Déco project inspired by the 1925 Paris Exposition, combining "streamlined moderne" details with industrial materials like Bakelite and aluminum. Divided into thirty sections, each separate space of the theater was designed with a specific decorative motif, enhanced with vibrant color, fabrics, balustrades, murals and sculpture, which, in line with the theme of the theater, celebrated the progress of man. The auditorium space is one of the largest in the world with a total seating capacity of about 6,200, and a stage 66.5 feet wide and 144 feet deep. The original hydraulic elevator equipment designed by Peter Clark is still in use today, and was the forerunner for international stage production, establishing a new standard in theatrical entertainment.

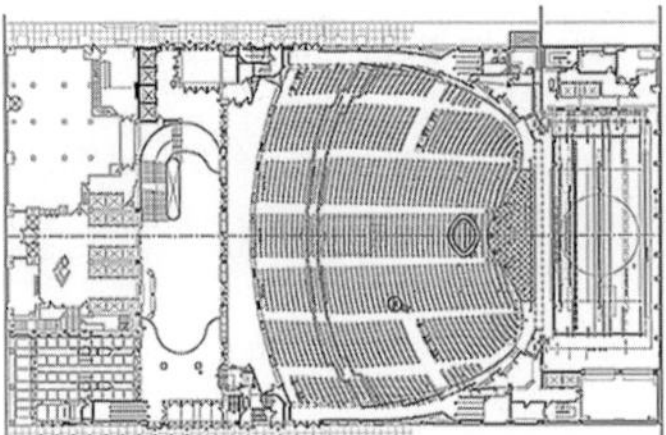

architects
Edward Durell Stone, Donald Deskey

type
theater

construction
1932

25. Museum of Modern Art – MoMA

11 W 53rd St
New York, NY 10019

Sat - Thu / 10.30 am - 5.30 pm
Fri / 10.30 am - 8.30 pm

+1 212 708 9400

www.moma.org

E > 5 Ave - 53 St station
B / D / F > 50 St - Rockefeller Center Station

BM1 / BM2 / BM4 / BM5 / SIM25 > 5 Ave - W 54 St

Founded in 1929, the MoMA is housed in a building that has constantly undergone regular changes, reflecting the continuous line of leading architects and the different stages in American architecture and international art, and with a collection in constant expansion. The museum began with 9 works, and today, it houses approximately 200,000 pieces. The permanent museum was designed by Philip Goodwin and Edward Durrell in 1939, based on the International Style, including an adjacent Sculpture Garden, designed by Philip Johnson (for many years director of the museum's Architecture Department). In 1984, César Pelli designed the first extension to the museum, composed of a tower set alongside the low original building. The most famous face of the museum was designed by Japanese architect, Yoshio Taniguchi, who completely transformed the internal and external space, incorporating the two adjacent buildings. A final radical project was assigned to Diller Scofidio + Renfro, who integrated innovative exhibition, technological, service and spatial solutions within a completely different MoMA structure.

architects
Philip Lippincott Goodwin, Edward Durell Stone / Philip Johnson / César Pelli / Yoshio Taniguchi / Diller Scofidio + Renfro

type
museum

construction
1939 / 1953 / 1984 / 2006 / 2019

26. 550 Madison Avenue

Madison Ave
New York, NY 10022

external viewing only

N / R / W > Lexington Ave - 59 St

QM21 > E 57 St - Park Ave
M1 / M2 / M3 / M4 > Madison Ave - E 56 St

The 550 Madison Avenue (also known as Sony Tower, originally the AT&T Building) stands out among the curtain wall facades on Madison Avenue because of its uniform cladding in pink granite. It is one of the most famous designs by Philip Johnson, who, despite having been awarded the Pritzker Architecture Prize in 1979 for his historical, analytical, and design contribution to modernist architecture, was experiencing a new prolific stage in his career: Postmodernism.
The 550 Madison Avenue is, in fact, the very first Postmodern design in New York on skyscraper scale, with a combination of diversified and decontextualized architectural trends. the design follows the symmetrical triple division of the classical column, with a base, shaft, and crowning element: an iconic pediment blending Neo-classical and Art Déco styles. The recent redevelopment project by the Norwegian firm, Snøhetta, plans to demolish the Neo-Romanesque style lobby, and encase the tall entrance archway and coffered ceiling with an undulated curtain wall of translucent glass to open up the building.

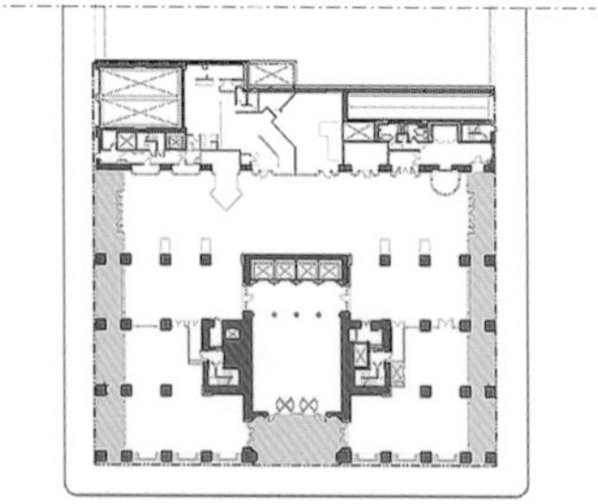

architects
Philip Johnson, John Burgee / Snøhetta

type
offices

construction
1984 / ongoing

27. 432 Park Avenue

432 Park Ave
New York, NY 10022

external viewing only

+1 212 432 2389
info@432parkavenue.com
www.432parkavenue.com

N / R / W > Lexington Ave - 59 St

QM21 > E 57 St - Park Ave
M1 / M2 / M3 / M4 > Madison Ave - E 56 St

The tall slender skyscraper at 432 Park Avenue is not only the tallest in Manhattan, but is also the highest residential building in the Western hemisphere. Designed by architect Rafael Viñoly, the 1,396 foot high building has a square footprint and the entire building is composed of a regular exposed concrete grid structure. This solution contributes to the building's identity and allows for internal space totally free of structural elements: large, light-filled, open-space rooms have views as far as Brooklyn. The structural grid squares measure approximately 10 × 10 feet, and the building is divided into six blocks, separated by filter floors, which are open and left exposed to the outdoor elements. These breaks allow for deflection of wind pressure and improve structural stability. The lower part of the building contains amenities for residents; these include a library, movie room, and indoor pool. The remaining 54 residential floors are reserved for luxury apartments, and a penthouse measuring over 8,255 square feet.

architects
Rafael Viñoly Architects

type
residential, retail

construction
2015

28. Louis Vuitton Store

1 E 57th St
New York, NY 10022

Mon - Sun / 10 am - 8 pm

+1 212 758 8877

www.us.louisvuitton.com

N / R / W > 5 Ave Station

M5, 32 > 5 Ave - W 58 St

A low building in Art Déco style on the corner of 5th Avenue and 57th Street has been home to one of the Louis Vuitton New York boutiques since 2002. The original building was designed by Cross&Cross in the 1930s and has undergone a number of alterations including the almost complete replacement of the original facade with white marble. This was integrated in 2004 with an elegant intervention by Japanese architect, Jun Aoki. Inspired by drawings by Hugh Ferris in 1929, the building almost seems to dissolve behind the glass facade that encloses the total structure. The moiré effect is obtained by a double layer of glass with an opaque white ceramic coating on the inner surface, while the outer surface is translucent and crystalline. The white area, used also as a neutral backdrop for temporary installations, creates a gradual transition from opacity to transparency with a white "Damier" pattern, the iconic Louis Vuitton motif introduced in 1888.

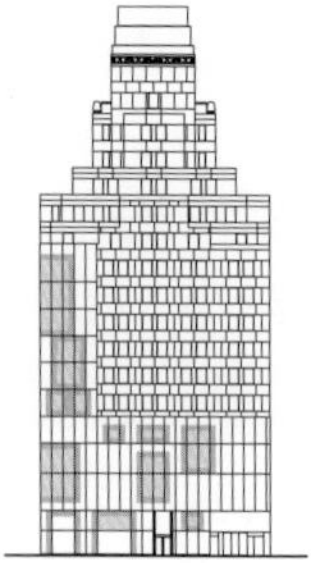

© Jun Aoki & Associates

architects
Jun Aoki & Associates

type
retail

construction
2004

29. Hearst Tower

301 W 56th St
New York, NY 10019

Mon - Fri / 10 am - 4 pm

+1 212 649 2000

www.hearst.com

1 / 2 / A / B / C / D >
59 St - Columbus Circle

M20 / M104 > 8 Ave -
W 56 St

The Hearst Tower was constructed to complete an early 1920s low-rise building designed by Joseph Urban for the Hearst Corporation which had remained uncompleted following the 1929 financial crisis. Its iconic jagged silhouette exceeds 590 feet in height, and Norman Foster was able to define an avant-garde solution that combined Art Déco architecture, high-tech design, and energy efficiency (it was the first building in Manhattan to be awarded LEED Gold certification).
An articulated modular structural frame encloses the whole building externally with a diagonal beam weave (diagrids), using far less steel than conventional construction systems; over 85% of the steel employed was derived from recycled material. The absence of any internal structure provides maximum flexibility throughout the 860 thousand foot internal floor space and optimizes the natural light. This has created 25% in energy savings, with integrated light sensor control systems and high performance energy materials. A rainwater recycling system is used to feed the theatrical waterfall sculpture that creates natural air cooling and humidification throughout the building.

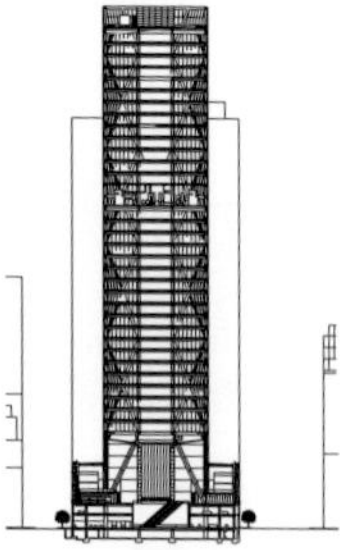

© Nigel Young / Foster + Partners

architects
Foster + Partners

type
offices

construction
2006

30. Time Warner Center

10 Columbus Circle
New York, NY 10019

Mon - Sat / 10 am - 9 pm
Sun / 11 am - 7 pm

+1 212 823 6300

www.
theshopsatcolumbuscircle.
com

1 / 2 / A / B / C / D >
59 St - Columbus Circle

M5 / M7 / M10 / M20
> Columbus Cir - 8 Ave

The Time Warner Center is a vast mixed-use complex that includes retail, residential and office space, as well as the Jazz Concert Hall of the nearby Lincoln Center, designed by Rafael Viñoly. This complex, created by Skidmore, Owings & Merrill, replaced a compact 1960s building, the New York Coliseum. It is composed of three geometrical blocks based on the existing urban layout, a solution that helped to visually reduce the imposing mass of the towers and the shadow they cast at street level. A multi-story concave podium covers the entire plot, following the curve of Columbus Circle towards the southwest corner of Central Park. It is divided in the center by a lower glazed portico that gives the visual impression that 59th Street passes through it. Laterally, the twin towers rise to a height of 750 feet, with parallelpiped bases designed to align them with Broadway and the right angle of 58th Street.

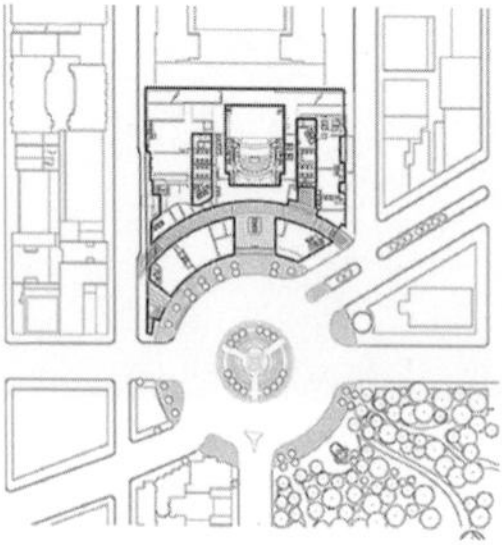

© Skidmore, Owings & Merrill

architects
Skidmore, Owings & Merrill

type
multi-purpose building

construction
2004

31. Mercedes House

550 W 54th St
New York, NY 10019

Mon - Thu / 10 am - 5 pm
Fri - Sat / 10 am - 6 pm
Sun / 11 am - 5 pm

+1 212 876 6666

www.mercedeshouseny.com

A / C / E > 50 St
Subway Station

Mercedes House is a residential and retail complex designed by the Mexican firm, TEN Arquitectos. It covers about 70% of a block in Hell's Kitchen. The complex is built in the form of a large stepped Z-shaped structure set on a low rectangular base, creating a clever morphological solution that reconciles the horizontal geography of the adjacent DeWitt Clinton Park with the vertical urban architecture of Midtown. Beginning at one end of 11th Avenue, the residential block rises in a regular step configuration, until it reaches triple height at the second facade. Each floor is the same height as the one below it, and provides a private green-roof terrace with a view of the Hudson River. This gives most of the 865 apartments the same levels of light and ventilation. The roof of the base podium building has been designed to serve as a usable outdoor space, composed of two large semi-public, well-equipped recreational areas, including a south-facing pool and a north-facing sports field. The podium building is completely dedicated to retail space with a 54,000 square foot Mercedes showroom.

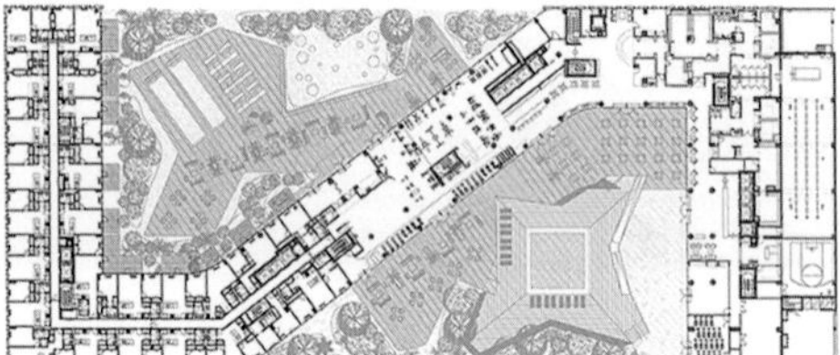

© TEN Arquitectos

architects
TEN Arquitectos

type
residential, retail

construction
2011

32. VIΛ 57 West

625 W 57th St
New York, NY 10019

open to the public

+1 646 630 7917

www.via57west.com

1 / 2 > 59 St - Columbus Circle

With VIΛ 57 West, the Danish firm founded by Bjarke Ingels, has introduced a new residential concept to Manhattan: the Courtscraper, a perfect cross between the density of the American Skyscraper and the internal courtyard, typical of European architecture. It has a rectangular footprint, but is composed of an irregular twisted pyramid shape that rises in the north-east corner to become a vertical axis 450 feet high. In perfect spatial and visual harmony with the surrounding urban context, the building opens out facing south towards the Hudson River, to take maximum advantage of natural sunlight and ventilation within the courtyard and internal spaces. On the roof, the horizontal ribbed sheeting is perforated in line with the terraces of each apartment, arranged in herringbone pattern. This is to provide south-facing exposure, and at the same time, guarantee privacy in all 709 apartments. The internal courtyard is a shared public space: a 22,000 square foot, lush, green garden that is a small-scale version of Central Park, with the same proportions.

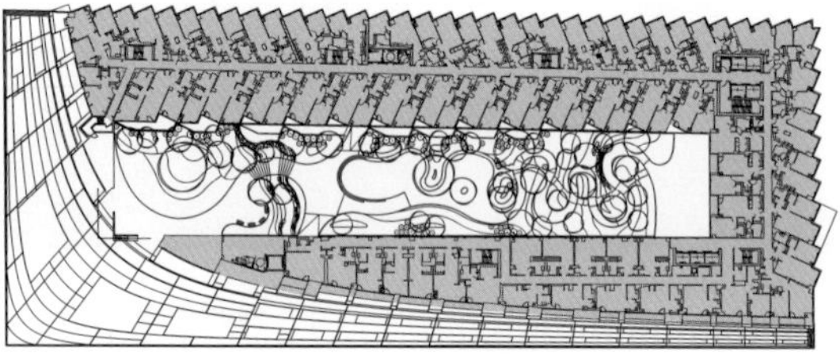

© Bjarke Ingels Group

© Iwan Baan

architects
Bjarke Ingles Group

type
residential

construction
2016

0 m
100 m
250 m
W 77th St
W 76th St
W 75th St
W 74th St
W 73rd St
W 72nd St
W 71st St
West End Ave
Broadway
W 79th St
W 78th St
W 80th St
W 79th St
W 78th St
W 77th St
W 76th St
W 75th St
W 74th St
W 81st
Columbus Ave
Amsterdam Ave
Beacon Theatre
40
39
W 77th St
New-York
Historical Society
72 St / Broadway
W 72nd St
W 71st St
W 70th St
W 69th St
W 67th St
W 66th St
W 75th St
W 74th St
W 73rd St
W 72nd St
W 71st St
W 70th St
W 69th St
W 68th St
W 67th St
W 66th St
W 65th St
W 64th St
Central Park West
The Dakota
72 St
Strawberry Fields
5
38
37
35
36
Lincoln Center
Theater
66 St - Lincoln
Center Subway
34
Metropolitan
Opera House
David Geffen Hall
33
Lincoln Center for
the Performing Arts
David H. Koch Theater
Adventure
Playground
Sheep Meadow
E

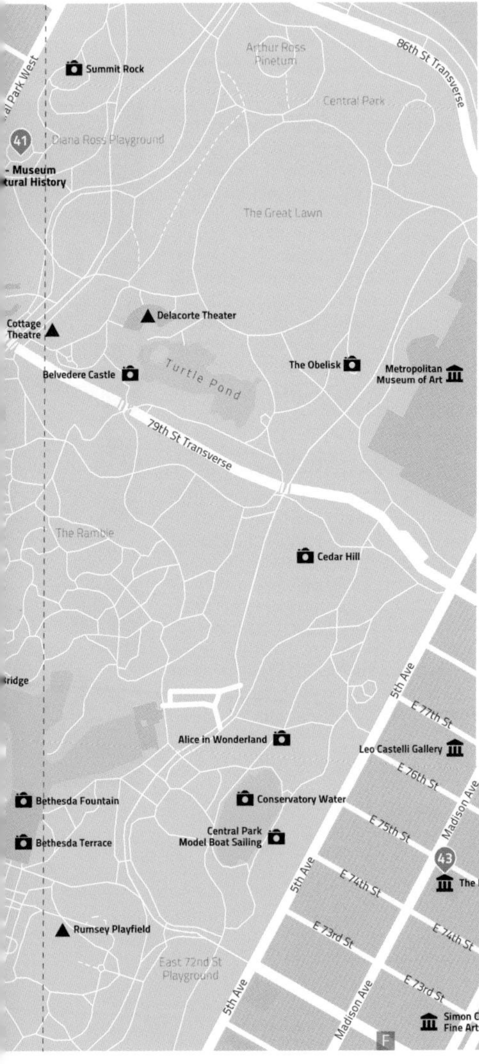

Upper Manhattan – Harlem

33. Lincoln Center for the Performing Arts
34. Metropolitan Opera House
35. Lincoln Center Theater
36. The Juilliard School
37. 170 Amsterdam
38. Lincoln Square Synagogue
39. American Museum of Natural History
40. Rose Center for Earth and Space
41. Central Park
42. Solomon R. Guggenheim Museum
43. The MET Breuer
44. The Diana Center – Barnard College
45. Manhattanville Campus
46. Roy and Diana Vagelos Education Center

33. Lincoln Center for the Performing Arts

Lincoln Center Plaza
New York, NY 10023

open to the public

+1 212 875 5456

www.lincolncenter.org

1 / 2 > 66 St - Lincoln Center

M11 > Columbus Ave - W 63 St
M104 > Broadway - W 63 St

The Lincoln Center occupies almost 17 acres on the West Side of Manhattan and is composed of different theaters and academic institutes. Promoted by Robert Moses and completed in 1966, it was the subject of considerable controversy because of the demolition of the San Juan Hill tenement district, famous as the setting for the film *West Side Story*. Wallace K. Harrison's master plan is a modernized version of Renaissance piazzas in Rome, with an EUR42 architectural style, just a block from Central Park. The heart of the Center is the Josie Robertson Plaza, by Philip Johnson, which strongly recalls Michelangelo's Piazza del Campidoglio. The twelve adjacent buildings were designed by different architects, but with a uniform height of about 98 feet, and are all clad in white Travertine stone from Tivoli, Rome.
The site and buildings have been undergoing large-scale renovation work since 2009, designed by Diller Scofidio + Renfro, who, as well as integrating technological solutions and landscape design, have created more usable space without altering the cohesion of the complex. The only new addition is the Hypar Pavilion, a low sloping structure with a green roof used by the public as a grassed pathway down to Hearst Plaza on the northern side.

architects
Wallace K. Harrison /
Diller Scofidio + Renfro

type
theater

construction
1964 / 2009

34. Metropolitan Opera House

30 Lincoln Center Plaza
New York, NY 10023

open to the public

+1 212 362 6000
MetropolitanOpera@
metopera.org
www.metopera.org

1 / 2 > 66 St - Lincoln Center

M11> Columbus Ave - W 63 St
M104 > Broadway - W 63 St

The Metropolitan Opera House was designed by Wallace K. Harrison, almost like a backdrop to the Josie Robertson Plaza. He designed 44 versions before reaching an agreement on the style and size with the Lincoln Center financiers. The MET is the largest opera house in the world with a seating capacity of 3,800, spread over 6 levels, and is the only theater in the Lincoln Center that did not need contemporary acoustic and performance equipment upgrades. It is composed of a box-like structure clad in travertine stone; the facade is graced with its distinctive five tall arches, behind which is a glass and bronze grid wall that reveals the two huge murals by Chagall in the full-height foyer which resembles projects by Eero Saarinen of the same period. The auditorium is fan-shaped and equipped with a highly mechanized rotating stage. The domed petal-shaped ceiling is covered with gold leaf squares and the walls are paneled in precious African wood noted for its acoustic quality.

architects
Wallace K. Harrison

type
theater

construction
1966

35. Lincoln Center Theater

150 W 65th St
New York, NY 10023

open to the public

+1 212 501 3100
access@lct.org.
www.lct.org

1 / 2 > 66 St - Lincoln Center

M11> Columbus Ave - W 63 St
M104 > Broadway - W 63 St

The Lincoln Center Theater is one of the last projects designed by the Finnish architect Eero Saarinen, completed after his death and created in collaboration with the stage-designer Jo Mielziner. It was the fourth building for the extension of the Center and is located opposite the Hearst Plaza; it features a pool by Mies van der Rohe and statue, *Reclining Figure* by British sculptor, Henry Moore. The project is a large rectangular block, accentuated by projecting roof clad in travertine stone, and supported by two strong pillars that flank the base, a glass box with slender steel framing. The building houses two auditoriums for theatrical performances.
In 2012, a third block, with a seating capacity of 112, the Claire Tow Theater, was added on the roof to stage contemporary theatrical performances. The Vivian Beaumont Theater is the largest auditorium with a seating capacity of 1,080 places, designed with an unusual horse-shoe layout that includes the stage but without a fore stage (technically: thrust stage). Below this theater on the basement floor, is the Mitzi Newhouse Theater, with a very flexible internal layout, and a maximum seating capacity of 299 seats.

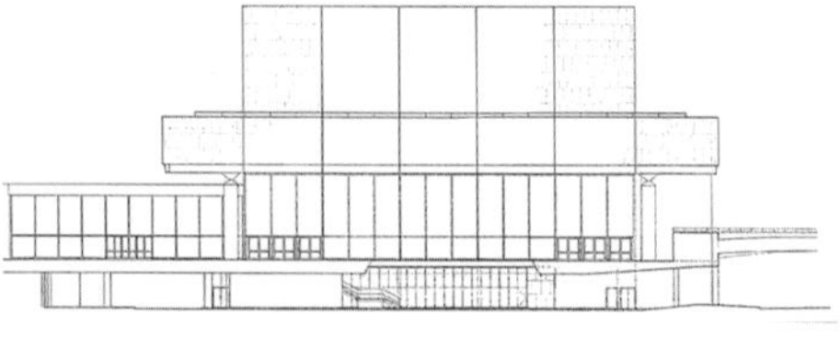

architects
Eero Saarinen, Jo Mielziner /
Hugh Hardy (extension)

type
theater

construction
1965 / 2012

36. The Juilliard School

1941 Broadway
New York, NY 10023

open to the public

+1 212 721 6500

www.lincolncenter.org

1 / 2 > 66 St - Lincoln Center

M11 > Columbus Ave - W 63 St
M104 > Broadway - W 63 St

The Juilliard School is the first American conservatory of performing arts, founded in 1920, and today one of the most important in the world. The current building, designed by Pietro Belluschi in the 1960s, has undergone the most extensive renovation interventions among the buildings in the recent Lincoln Center redevelopment and expansion plans. The closer, tighter interior layout was modified to create much larger spaces and more common areas. The travertine facades were sliced at the base level and replaced by glass walls to improve the visual and spatial connection between the Lincoln center complex and Juilliard, positioned at the northernmost part of the site. The previous lobby area has been almost doubled with the demolition of the facade and the addition of a new cantilevered extension, respecting the angle of Broadway. This choice was made to preserve the height limit of the complex. The glass section slope is repeated in the plaza in front of the school, with steps leading to the lobby of the Alice Tully Hall, which has been completely redesigned.

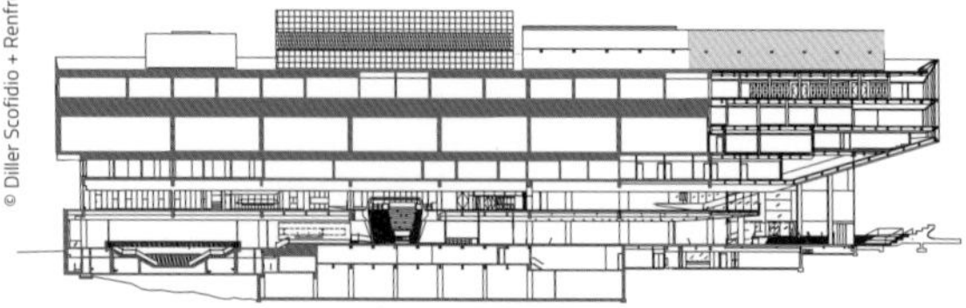

© Diller Scofidio + Renfro

architects
Pietro Belluschi /
Diller Scofidio + Renfro
(restoration, extension)

type
education

construction
1969 / 2009

37. 170 Amsterdam

170 Amsterdam Ave
New York, NY 10023

external viewing only

+1 646 601 7257

www.equityapartments.com

1 / 2 > 72 St - Broadway

M11 > Amsterdam Ave - W 69 St

Walking along along Amsterdam Avenue, it is impossible not to notice the Handel Architects project at number 170. A visibly light, reinforced concrete exoskeleton encloses the glass walls that are set back about 15 centimeters and horizontally divided by narrow exposed slabs. The skeleton intersects at various heights and extends in a right angle onto the roof terrace used for condominium services. The diagrid structural solution was created using a particular system of tubular beams cast in specifically constructed form-work and a mix of light gray concrete that resembles the limestone used on surrounding buildings, giving the facades a dynamic effect typical of the projecting cornices and balconies on apartment buildings on the Upper West Side. The external framework also provides adequate structural rigidity to maximize the internal usable space in this building that occupies almost the whole rectangular city block.

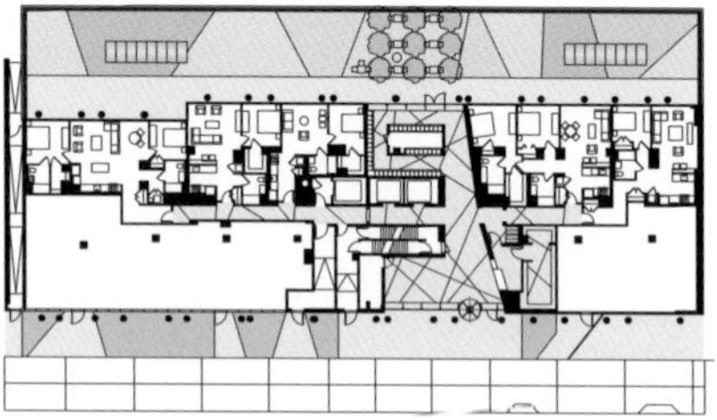

© Handel Architects

architects
Handel Architects

type
residential

construction
2015

38. Lincoln Square Synagogue

180 Amsterdam Ave
New York, NY 10023

open to the public

+1 212 874 6100

www.lss.org

1 / 2 > 72 St - Broadway

M11 > Amsterdam Ave - W 69 St

Founded in 1964 in an apartment on the Upper West Site, today, the Lincoln Square Synagogue is an important institution for modern New York Orthodox Judaism. In order to cater to a strongly expanding community, the current synagogue was designed by CetraRuddy to coordinate spiritual values, imagery and references to Jewish worship. The architectural layout and materials were chosen to reflect the symbolic perception of the five books of the Torah. The five-story synagogue has an open plan concept to provide a collective area in the center and secondary spaces surrounding it. On the ground floor, the circular sanctuary space can accommodate 442 people and is designed with sloping undulated walls to amplify the acoustics, since electric sound amplifiers are not used during prayer hours. 613 light points in the ceiling represent the 613 Jewish commandments (*mitzvòt*).
The street facade is composed of five undulating bands of glass and bronze colored fabric panels, to recall the sacred scrolls, flanked at each end by two monolithic stone elements.

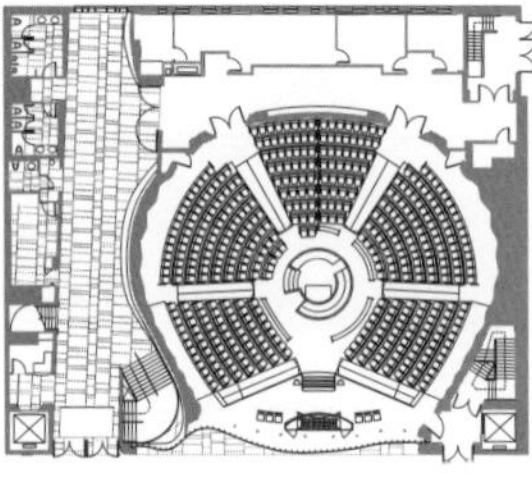

© CetraRuddy Architecture

© David Sundberg/Esto

architects
CetraRuddy

type
place of worship

construction
2013

39. American Museum of Natural History

Central Park W 79th St
New York, NY 10024

Mon - Sun / 10 am - 5.45 pm

+1 212 769 5100
communications@amnh.org
www.amnh.org

B / C > 81 St - Museum of Natural History
1 > 79th St

Ever since its foundation in 1869, the American Museum of Natural History has been one of the greatest institutions in the world in the field of museum diffusion of scientific research. It covers four blocks along the west side of Central Park, and was originally a Victorian Gothic style building designed by Calvert Vaux, later modified and expanded in Beaux Arts style with a new monumental entrance. In the 1990s, the architect, Kevin Roche, who was responsible for the architectural maintenance of the museum, carried out numerous interventions to modernize the technical services and increase internal space. He also expanded the library with a new additional 8-story building.
The most recent radical expansion project, the Gilder Center, was assigned to Studio Gang and will be completed in 2022 with the construction of a 754,000 square foot building with an innovative design based on the liquid properties of concrete to create a continuous fluid curvilinear concept for both the external facade and the interior space.

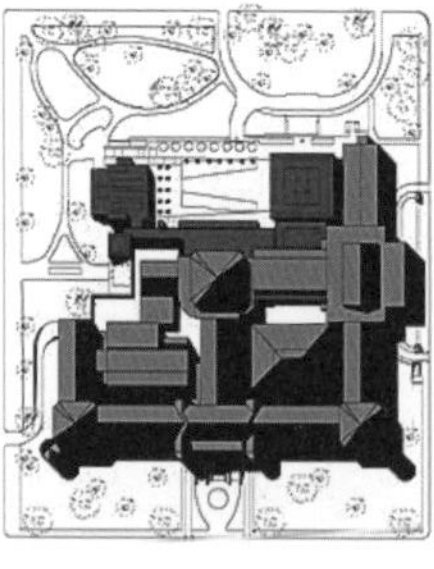

architects
Calvert Vaux / Josiah Cleavcland Cady (extension) / Kevin Roche John Dinkeloo and Associate (library) / Studio Gang (extension)

type
museum

construction
1877 / 1935 / 1992 / ongoing

40. Rose Center for Earth and Space

208 79th St
New York, NY 10024

Mon - Sun / 10 am - 5.45 pm

+1 212 769 5100

www.amnh.org

A / B / C > 81 St - Museum of Natural History Station

M69 / SBS > W 81 Street - Central Park West
M10 > Central PK W - W 79 St

The Rose Center for Earth and Space was founded in 1933 in the northern sector of the American Museum of Natural History. It houses research areas, laboratories and exhibition space covering an area of over 333,500 square feet. The central element of the complex is the Hayden Planetarium, realized thanks to a donation made in 1935 by the philanthropist, Charles Hayden, although it has been demolished and redesigned several times because of the constant advances in astrophysics and technology. The current project was designed in 2000 by James Polshek, who is now a member of Ennead Architects. The building is composed of two pure volumes: an enormous glass cube with a grid structure, that houses an 87 foot sphere. Clearly visible from the large plaza in front of the center, the white sphere seems to float on its solid structural truss work embedded in a basement floor. It is surrounded by a spiral ramp that narrates the exploration of the history of the universe, rising up to the Star Theater, where the full-dome video system visualizes current astrophysical data in real time giving viewers a full immersion learning experience.

© Jeff Goldberg / Esto

architects
Polshek Partnership

type
museum

construction
2000

41. Central Park

Central Park
New York, NY

Mon - Sun / 6 am - 1 am

+1 212 310 6600
info@centralparknyc.org
www.centralparknyc.org

A / B / C > 110 St - Cathedral Pkwy Station / 103 St / 96 St / 86 St / 81 St - Museum of Natural History Station / 72 St / 59 St - Columbus Circle /
D > 59 St - Columbus Circle
F / M > 57 St
N / R / W > 5 Av
1 / 2 > 59 St - Columbus Circle
2 / 3 > 110 St Station - Central Park North

Central Park is a vast green rectangle that covers 843 acres between Midtown and Harlem, and creates a rupture in the tight residential weave of Uptown Manhattan. Originally the park was not planned in the geometrical division of the grid, and became a fundamental episode in the urban and social history of the city. It was built between 1853 and 1876, as a result of a public landscape design competition to bring a corrective element to the homogeneous urban layout lacking in green spaces. It was directed at taking best advantage of the ground and the air, as well as an experiment in democratization able to connect districts and neighborhoods of very different social classes, lifestyles, and architectural styles. Although the topography and woodland areas seem natural, Central Park is an impressive man-made product, perhaps the only urban object in New York that was completely planned in every practical and formal detail. The whole landscape was remodeled, layered, and constructed artificially to create a natural environment; even the soil was not suitable for planting, and was transported in from New Jersey. Central Park is the fifth largest park in New York city. It is one of the most popular tourist attractions in the United States, and above all one of the favorite places for all New Yorkers.

architects	type	construction
Frederick Law Olmsted	park	1857 - 1876

The 19th century layout has remained practically unchanged although the park has added numerous attractions and facilities over the years to cater to cultural events and concerts (mainly concentrated in the Great Lawn area). The park is home to about 4 million trees, shrubs and plants including numerous non-native species, and a large number of mammals and migrating birds. Within the park, the area most often visited is the Strawberry Fields Garden dedicated to the memory of John Lennon.

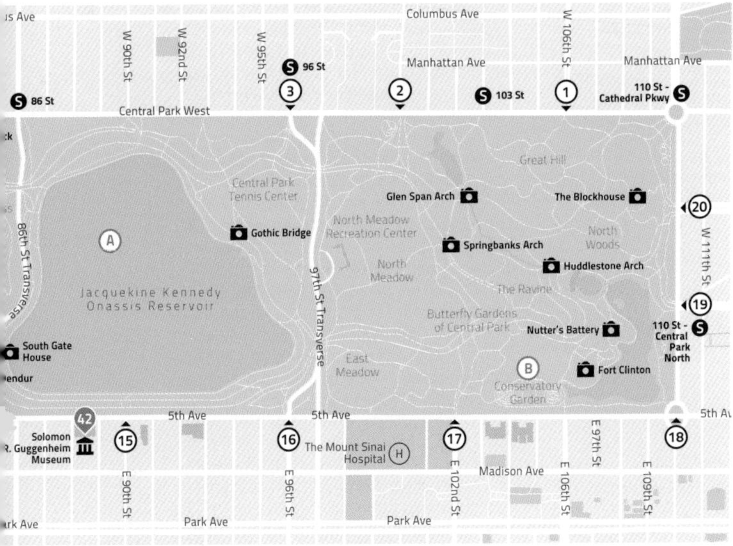

A. Jacqueline Kennedy Onassis Reservoir
B. Conservatory Garden
C. Shakespeare Garden
D. The Ramble
E. Alice in Wonderland
F. Bethesda Terrace
G. The Mall and Literary Walk
H. Central Park Carousel
I. Sheep Meadow
J. Strawberry Fields Memorial
K. Bow Bridge

1. Strangers' Gate / W 106th St
2. Boys' Gate / W 100th St
3. Gate of all Saints / W 96th St
4. Mariners' Gate / W 85th St
5. Hunters' Gate / W 81st St
6. Naturalists' Gate / W 77th St
7. Womens' Gate / W 72nd St
8. Merchants' Gate / Columbus Circle
9. Artisans' Gate / 7th Ave
10. Artists' Gate / 6th Ave
11. Scholars' Gate / E 60th St
12. Childrens' Gate / E 64th St
13. Inventors' Gate / E 72nd St
14. Miners' Gate / E 79th St
15. Engineers' Gate / E 90th St
16. Woodman's Gate / E 96th St
17. Girls' Gate / E 102nd St
18. Pioneers' Gate / E 110th St
19. Farmers' Gate / Lenox Ave
20. Warriors' Gate / Adam Clayton Powell Blvd

42. Solomon R. Guggenheim Museum

1071 5th Ave
New York, NY 10128

Mon, Wed - Fri, Sun /
10 am - 17.30 pm
Tue, Sat / 10 am - 8.30 pm

+1 212 423 3500
boxoffice@guggenheim.org
www.guggenheim.org

4 / 5 / 6 > 86 St
Station

M1 / M2 / M3 / M4 >
5 Ave - E 90 St

The Guggenheim Museum in New York is considered one of the most important examples of modern architecture in the world, and the peak of the final stage of Frank Lloyd Wright's career. Solomon R. Guggenheim commissioned Wright to design the building in 1943 as the permanent site for the Guggenheim Foundation and its expanding collection of modern art, but neither man was present at the inauguration in 1959.
The request for a completely new museum concept inspired the first steps of a project in the 1920s for the Gordon Strong Planetarium, which was never built. Set among the skyscrapers of Manhattan on the edge of Central Park, the Guggenheim Museum is a low white cylindrical structure, compact and monochromatic, without external openings. Inside, overhead light floods in from a vast glass dome over the full height circular atrium. Around the perimeter, a spiral ramp gives the idea of "one great space on a continuous floor" to form a single linear gallery without interruption.
An extension, designed by Gwathmey Siegel, was built in 1992, based on the original drawings which had included a rectangular ten-story tower on the north-eastern side.

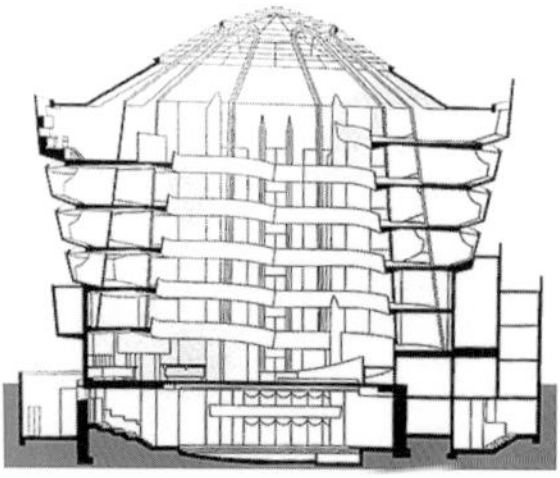

architects
Frank Lloyd Wright

type
museum

construction
1939

43. The MET Breuer

945 Madison Ave
New York, NY 10021

Tue - Thu, Sun /
10 am - 5.30 pm
Fri - Sat / 10 am - 9 pm

+1 212 731 1675

www.metmuseum.org

4 / 6 > 77 St

M1 / M2 / M3 / M4 >
Madison Ave - E 75 St

When walking down Madison Avenue, the MET Breuer appears as an unusual monolithic, granite clad block, in stark contrast to the brick buildings of the Upper East Side. Originally designed in 1966 as the Whitney Museum of American Art, the museum is now part of the Metropolitan Museum of Art who named it after its designer: Marcel Breuer.

This is a compact sculptural design, with a strong Brutalist influence, but with a strict spatial functionalist approach at the same time. It is composed of a dense concrete block, perforated by trapezoidal projecting windows, which rises in graduated overlapping sections like an inverted ziggurat. Inside the building, the heavy concrete elements are molded with care to obtain a diverse range of surfaces from bush-hammered effects to concrete mixed with reflective obsidian chips. The four upper floors form open-space exhibition galleries with prefabricated concrete coffered ceilings that encase a track system for creating sliding partitions and directing lighting.

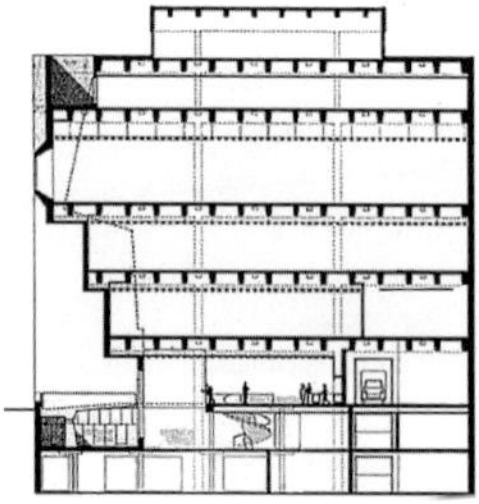

architects
Marcel Breuer / Beyer Blinder Belle (restoration)

type
museum

construction
1966 / 2016

44. The Diana Center – Barnard College

3009 Broadway
New York, NY 10027

Mon - Sun / 9 am - 5 pm

+1 212 854 5262

www.barnard.edu

1 > 116 St Station - Columbia University

M104 > Broadway - W 119 St
M5 > Riverside Dr - W 119 St

Founded in 1889 as a women's college, part of the famous Columbia University, Barnard College occupies a secondary campus located along Broadway. It is composed of a group of traditional red brick buildings, and was recently expanded in 2010 with a multi-use center designed by Weiss/Manfredi. The Diana Center unites interior and exterior in a seven-story building that has become the new social, cultural, and intellectual center for campus life, featuring a dynamic layering of previously separate research programs. It is composed of a wedge-shaped structure with a diagonal void carved through the building. Stepped level floors are connected by a system of double height terraced levels. The glazed cantilevered route rises from the atrium up a continuous unfolded staircase that connects all floors as far as the green-roof equipped for biological research. The facade, composed of 1,154 clear, translucent, and color integral glass panels, provides calibrated light according to the needs of the internal space. The integral glass stripes recall the red brick color of the surrounding buildings.

architects
Weiss/Manfredi

type
college

construction
2010

45. Manhattanville Campus

605 W 129th St
New York, NY 10027

open to the public

+1 212 854 5915
communityaffairs@columbia.edu
www.manhattanville.columbia.edu

1 > 125 St

M4 > Broadway - W 129 St

Columbia University is building its second campus in the Manhattanville ex-industrial area in West Harlem to expand its historic Morningside Heights campus. The master plan was assigned to Renzo Piano Building Workshop in collaboration with Skidmore, Owings & Merrill, and should be completed before 2030. The aim is to open up one of the most important universities in the world and integrate it within the existing urban and social context. The permeable, hybrid, spatial and functional concept will create a complete metamorphosis; the campus will become an active part of the neighborhood, without physical barriers, and will connect with the surrounding pedestrian and traffic system where plazas and green public spaces will be integrated. Similarly, the ground levels of all buildings will be open to public access to create a widespread urban area destined for recreational activities and services for the community. Piano also designed the first four buildings on the southernmost end of the campus site cut by Broadway. Three are already completed: The Forum, the Lenfest Center for the Arts and the Jerome L. Greene Science Center, which will be followed in 2021 by two buildings for the Columbia Graduate School of Business designed by Diller Scofidio + Renfro.

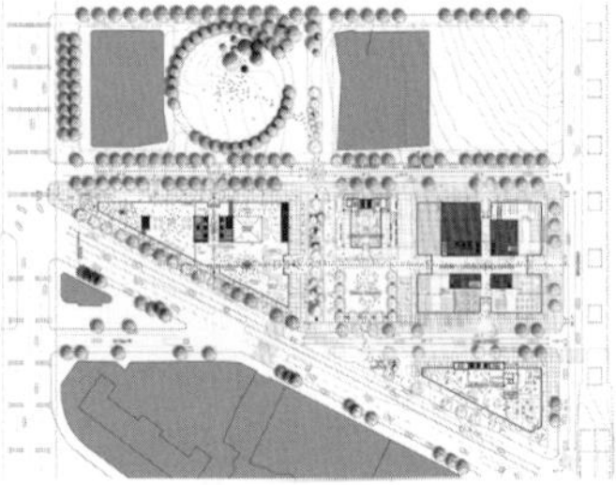

architects
Renzo Piano Building Workshop; Skidmore, Owings & Merrill / Renzo Piano Building Workshop

type
campus

construction
2007 / 2018 - ongoing

46. Roy and Diana Vagelos Education Center

104 Haven Ave
New York, NY 10032

Mon - Fri / 8 am - 5 pm

+1 212 305 2862

www.ps.columbia.edu

A > 175 St Station

M4 > Ft Washington Ave - W 172 St

The Roy and Diana Vagelos Education Center is one of the medical research centers of Columbia University. The project, the result of painstaking research conducted by Diller Scofidio + Renfro on holistic medical teaching, established an innovative institutional model, open and dynamic, to cover specific needs linked to technologically advanced research, encouraging collaboration between four different university courses.
On the south side, a continuous staircase rises from the lobby connecting informal and communal areas arranged over 14 floors. This spreads over every level and contains a vast range of spaces including a 275-seating capacity auditorium, outdoor terraces, individual study alcoves, collective areas designed with flexible partitions and integrated screens that can be pulled down from the false ceilings. The dense zig-zag structure, visible from the exterior, becomes the visual as well as social focus of the urban context in Washington Heights.

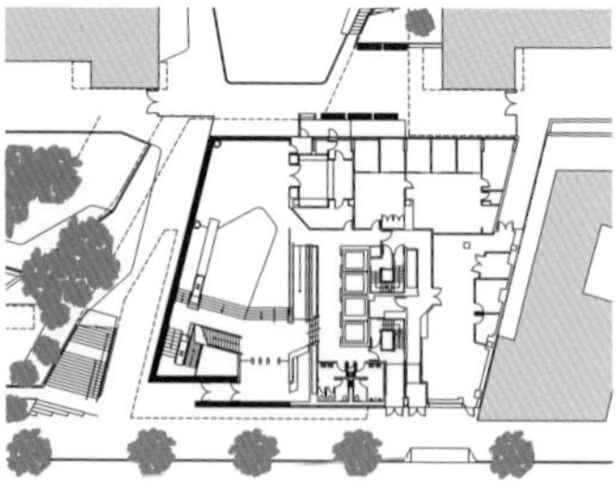

© Diller Scofidio + Renfro

architects
Diller Scofidio + Renfro,
Gensler

type
research center

construction
2016

Lower Manhattan

47. The Whitney Museum of American Art
48. The New School University Center
49. 41 Cooper Square
50. Bayard-Condict Building
51. Sperone Westwater Gallery
52. New Museum
53. Prada Epicenter
54. Scholastic Inc. Building
55. 565 Broome Soho
56. 56 Leonard Street
57. The Woolworth Building
58. The Fulton Center
59. The Oculus – World Trade Center Transportation Hub
60. Four World Trade Center
61. 9/11 Memorial Pavilion
62. National September 11 Memorial
63. One World Trade Center
64. Statue of Liberty Museum
65. The Hills

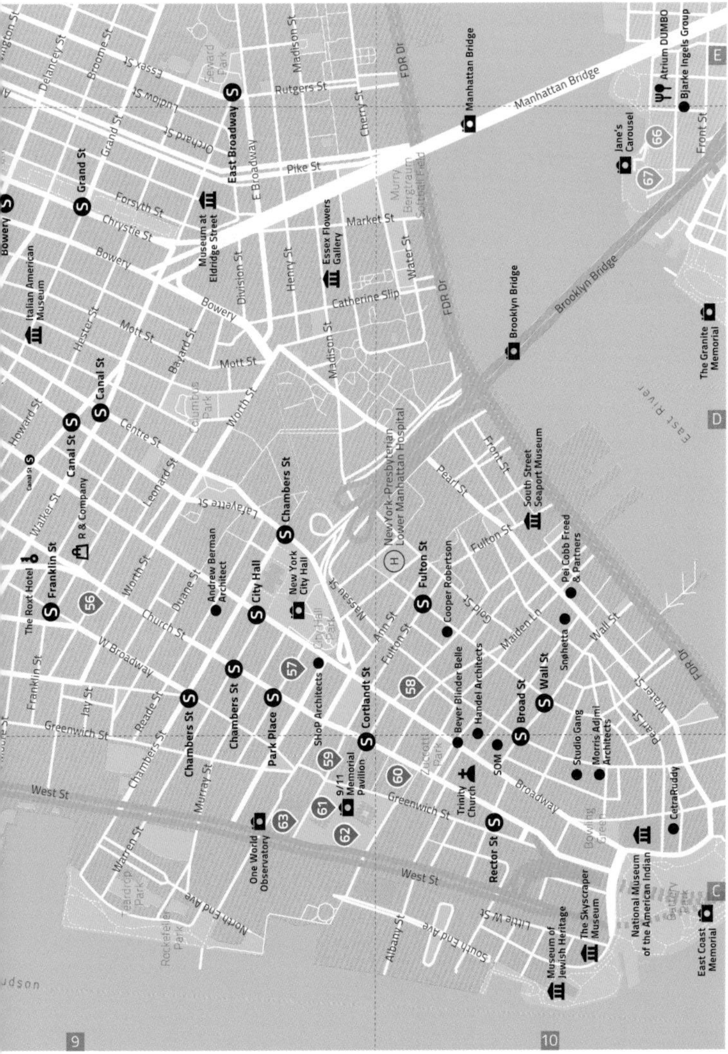

Bowery
Italian American Museum
Grand St
Museum at Eldridge Street
East Broadway
Essex Flowers Gallery
Manhattan Bridge
Canal St
R & Company
The Roxt Hotel
Franklin St
56
Andrew Berman Architect
City Hall
Chambers St
New York City Hall
NewYork-Presbyterian Lower Manhattan Hospital
Fulton St
Cooper Robertson
South Street Seaport Museum
Pei Cobb Freed & Partners
Snøhetta
Wall St
Broad St
Handel Architects
Beyer Blinder Belle
SOM
Trinity Church
Rector St
57
SHoP Architects
Park Place
Cortlandt St
58
59
60
61
62
63
9/11 Memorial Pavilion
One World Observatory
Studio Gang
Morris Adjmi Architects
CetraRuddy
National Museum of the American Indian
The Skyscraper Museum
Museum of Jewish Heritage
East Coast Memorial
The Granite Memorial
Brooklyn Bridge
Jane's Carousel
66
67
Atrium DUMBO
Bjarke Ingels Group
East River
Hudson
9
10
C
D
E

47. The Whitney Museum of American Art

99 Gansevoort St
New York, NY 10014

Mon - Wed - Thu - Sun /
10.30 am - 6 pm
Fri - Sat / 10.30 am - 10 pm

+1 212 570 3600
info@whitney.org
www.whitney.org

1 / 2 / 3 / A / C / E / L
> 14 St Station

M11 > Greenwich St -
Horatio St

The Whitney Museum of American Art expanded its historic exhibition space in 2015 with a project designed by Renzo Piano Building Workshop in collaboration with Cooper Robertson. The museum was commissioned to accommodate their ever-increasing collection of American modern and contemporary art, previously housed in the iconic building designed by Marcel Breuer in Madison Avenue. The new museum, located in the Meatpacking District, occupies a site adjacent to the famous High Line park and the west bank of the Hudson River. The highly dynamic, asymmetrical construction follows the geometry of the site and is cleverly integrated with its surrounding urban context. The view from the opposite side of the Hudson shows the diversified and irregular structure that harmonizes well with the New York skyline.
The ground floor of the museum forms a large public plaza roofed by an imposing cantilevered projection that welcomes and protects, while extending towards a space that visually connects the limits of the city on one hand, and the river on the other, with the interior of the structure. As well as the five floors of exhibition space, the museum also houses a large theater. The museum is not only an outstanding exhibition space, but is also one of the most dynamic cultural and artistic hubs in New York.

© RPBW

architects
Renzo Piano Building
Workshop, Cooper Robertson

type
museum

construction
2015

48. The New School University Center

63 5th Ave
New York, NY 10003

open to the public

+1 212 229 5600

www.newschool.edu

F / L > 14 St Station

M14A / M14D > W 14 St - 5 Av

The New School University Center, of which Skidmore, Owings & Merrill also designed the interior and completed in 2014, represents not only a new ethical project design based on low environmental impact, but above all, an interesting new concept for university structures in general. The innovative aspect of the project is the idea of combining many different functions, that are normally compartmentalized, within the same building, creating an interesting cultural hybrid concept. The lower floors of the building, occupied by classrooms, meeting rooms, library, study areas, cafes and space for academic and leisure activities, is integrated into the dense New York grid system, and presents a mainly horizontal facade. This is interrupted transversely, showing the articulated internal distribution system, creating a strong link between the university campus and public spaces. The upper floors, with a more enclosed, private facade, house the student dormitories, that are located below the technical and service areas, on the top of the building. This complex has been designed to combine a series of different functions with learning, living, dining, and socializing spaces for students. It provides a complete campus system within a single building for future generations.

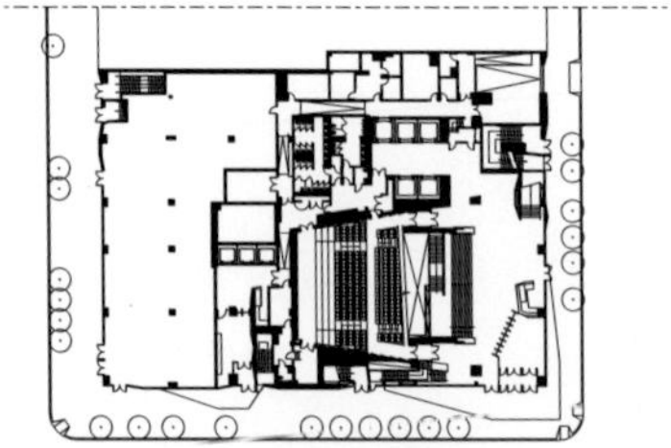

© Skidmore, Owings & Merrill

architects
Skidmore, Owings & Merrill

type
education

construction
2014

49. 41 Cooper Square

41 Cooper Sq
New York, NY 10003

external viewing only

+1 212 353 4100
webmaster@cooper.edu
www.cooper.edu

B / D / F / L >
Broadway - Lafayette
St Station

M103 > Cooper Sq
E - E 6 St

41 Cooper Square, the main academic building of The Cooper Union, houses the school's engineering department alongside facilities for art and design to encourage cross-disciplinary dialogue. Located in Cooper Square, it was designed by Morphosis and built between 2006 and 2009. The architects' aim was to create an iconic morphological design with great impact to embody the university's values and aspirations as a center for advanced education. In this sense, the exterior of the building that covers the whole site, merges with the interior through a vertical plaza, created by a 20-foot wide grand staircase which climbs four stories from the ground level to the full height of the building, forming the central space for informal social, intellectual and creative exchange. The multiple roles of this building are most clearly seen on the ground floor which symbolically welcomes the city into the foyer with a series of public functions. The constant search for innovative ideas can be seen in the green building technologies that have made this university facility highly sustainable. This project is aimed at shining a light on the university's legacy of innovation and creative practices, and its extremely original design is a perfect reflection of this concept.

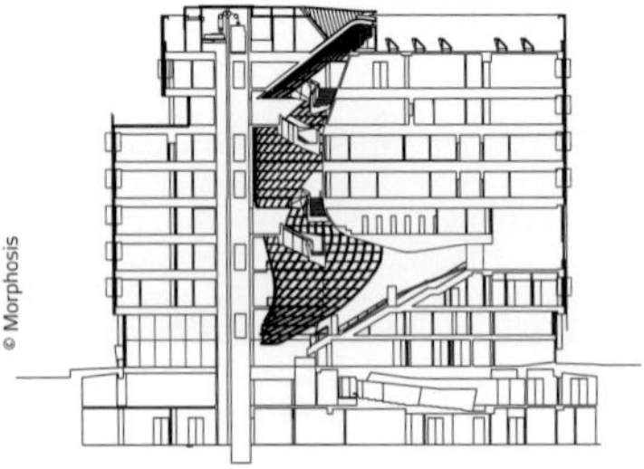

© Morphosis

architects
Morphosis

type
education

construction
2009

50. Bayard-Condict Building

65 Bleecker St
New York, NY 10012

external viewing only

4 / 6 / B / D / F > Bleecker St - Lafayette St

M1 > Lafayette St - E Houston St

Among the vast production of works by Louis Sullivan, considered as "the father of Modernism", the Bayard-Condict Building represents not only one of the most radical architectural projects of the period, but it is also the only building in New York designed by this famous American architect. The structure is clearly defined in three sections: the base for public use, the shaft for office space, and the crown, richly decorated with friezes to support the cornice. This historic landmark is an authentic manifesto of the design concept of the School of Chicago, of which Sullivan was a leading figure. The facade shows the use of the innovative steel frame structure elegantly concealed by the ornamental terracotta cladding. The ordered arrangement of the vertical elements in contrast with the horizontal spandrels on the facade give an impression of extended verticality to a building design that is, in fact, quite compact. The effect is coherent with Sullivan's other works, recognized forerunners of the most representative style of American architectural design in the early 20th century: the skyscraper.

architects
Louis Sullivan

type
offices

construction
1899

51. Sperone Westwater Gallery

257 Bowery
New York, NY 10002

Tue - Sat / 10 am - 6 pm

+1 212 999 7337

www.speronewestwater.com

B / D / F > Broadway - Lafayette St Station
J > Bowery Station

M103 > Bowery - Prince St

The Sperone Westwater Gallery, is a prestigious contemporary art museum and a prominent artistic structure in the Bowery. In 2010, the gallery space was increased with an innovative project by the London architects, Foster + Partners. The building occupies a typical regular New York grid site, but has invented a new way for the public to engage with art in a museum setting. The Bowery Street facade is composed of a plain wall of milled glass, divided by regular grid framing. The innovative feature is a moving room that glides up and down the first five floors of the building's exhibition spaces; these are separated from the private office spaces located in the upper floor setback structure. The moving room gives the public a new viewing experience by stopping on a level with each exhibition space, connecting with it, and provides a means for constantly changing, expanding, and building new exhibition spaces. The milled glass facade provides a sharp contrast between the dynamic intensity of the city and the reflective tranquility of the gallery, allowing viewers to distance themselves while viewing the artworks inside the museum, and at the same time, represents the tangible fluidity of the world of art in our contemporary existence.

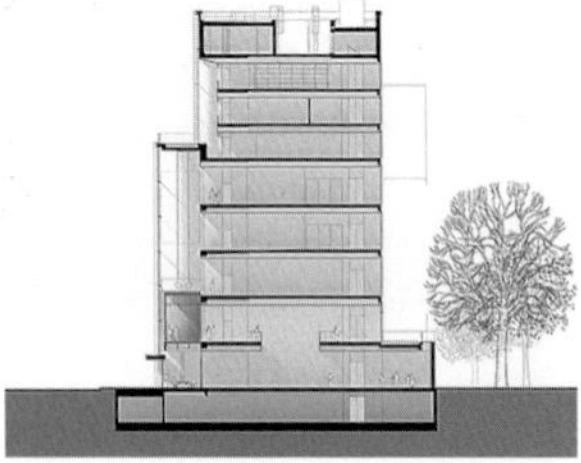

© Foster + Partners

architects
Foster + Partners

type
art gallery

construction
2010

52. New Museum

235 Bowery
New York, NY 10002

Tue - Wed / 11 am - 6 pm
Thu / 11 am - 9 pm
Fri - Sun / 11 am - 6 pm

+1 212 219 1222
info@newmuseum.org
www.newmuseum.org

B / D / F > Broadway - Lafayette St Station
J > Bowery Station

M103 > Bowery - Prince St

The New Museum of Contemporary Art, opened in 2007, is the only New York museum devoted exclusively to showing international contemporary art; it was designed by the Japanese architects, Kazuyo Sejima and Ryue Nishizawa, founders of the SANAA architectural firm. The museum was constructed on a typical New York site, with a regular perimeter, and with existing buildings on each side. It was because of these limits that the architects decided how to develop the project: the museum is composed of the repetitive stacking of seven 'boxes', to recall the regular building-block style typical of Lower Manhattan. When stacked on top of one another and shifted to one side or another, the displaced boxes define the configuration and give the building dynamic impact, as well as allowing adequate natural light to filter into the building. The effect is innovative, but at the same time, familiar within the geometrical narrative of the context surrounding the museum, because all formal references were eliminated. A project to extend the exhibition space was designed by the Dutch firm, OMA, with a strong focus on the entrance and link with the public, continuing the pure clean lines of the SANAA concept, although in a different style.

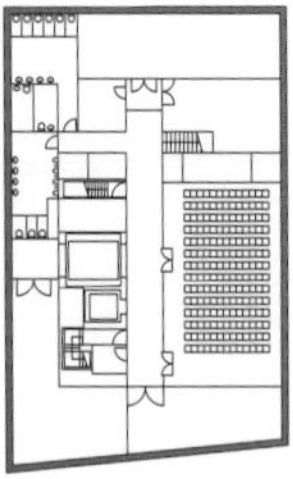

© SANAA

architects
SANAA / OMA

type
museum

construction
2007 / ongoing

53. Prada Epicenter

575 Broadway
New York, NY 10012

Mon - Sun / 11 am - 7 pm

+1 212 334 8888

www.prada.com

N / Q / R / W > Prince St Station
B / D / F / M > Broadway - Lafayette St Station

SIM7 / SIM9 / SIM33 > W Houston St - Mercer St

Ever since its opening in 2011, the Prada Epicenter, designed by the Dutch firm, OMA, and overseen by Rem Koolhaas in close collaboration with Miuccia Prada, has represented not only an innovative and unusual approach to architecture for fashion, but also, and above all, has created an unprecedented experience between customers and consumer retail spaces. In this project, defined as an intentionally hybrid space because of the relationship between the various functions and designations, the distinguishing element in the store is the so-called "Wave", a wooden structure about 196 feet long, that merges sinuously inside the space that previously formed the separation between two floors. And that is not all. The curved surface at street level, is scooped out of the ground floor, opening it up to the basement level; the structure can be modified to provide a range of different functions, from the presentation of new collections, to art performances, making the space unique in the architectural panorama linked with fashion, art and culture.

© OMA

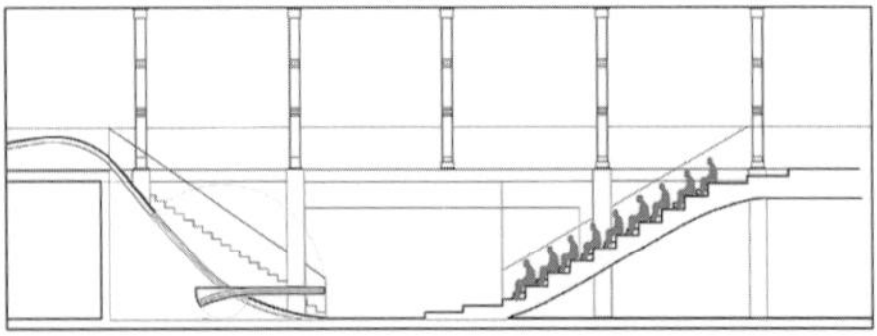

architects
OMA

type
retail

construction
2001

54. Scholastic Inc. Building

557 Broadway
New York, NY 10012

Mon - Fri / 9 am - 5 pm

+1 800 724 6527

www.scholastic.com

R / W > Prince St
6 > Spring St
B / D / F / M >
Broadway Lafayette

M1 / M55 >
Broadway - Prince St

The building for the Scholastic Inc. publishing company, designed by Aldo Rossi and built after his death by Morris Adjimi in 2001, is a demonstration of his close adherence to the theoretical principles of the famous Italian architect. Built on a typical SoHo site, characterized by the dense grid layout with access from only two street fronts, the building has two facades, with distinct hierarchical order. The main facade on Broadway appears with all its literal and metaphorical links to early 19th century New York architectural history. Firstly, in the modular structural scansion of the facade that clearly recalls the three-sectioned construction composed of base, shaft and crown; secondly in the choice of materials, in particular, steel, stone, and terracotta, the principal materials used by the School of Chicago; and lastly in the construction method based on the use of prefabricated parts assembled on site. The facade on Mercer Street takes on the appearance of a service entrance with a more industrial style, emphasized by the lattice structure and cast iron elements. However, it maintains Rossi's persistent and everlasting rules of proportion, able to convey a strong powerful message in all elements of the project through his meticulous and restrained method of architectural design and construction.

architects
Aldo Rossi / Morris Adjmi
Architects (realization)

type
offices

construction
2001

55. 565 Broome Soho

565 Broome St
New York, NY 10013

external viewing only

+1 212 355 0565
info@565broomesoho.com
www.565broomesoho.com

1 / 2 > Canal St Station
A / C / E > Spring St Subway Station

M55 > Ave of the Americas - Broome St

The first project by Renzo Piano Building Workshop for a residential building in New York, at 565 Broome Street, represents an innovative approach in the field of residential towers in the city. The 290 foot tall, 30-story building, has an unusual concept, in which the structure above the podium base is separated into two twin parallel towers. This separation of a single block into two vertical elements reduces the impression of a predominant mass and improves the proportions of the overall view. It also resolves the question of the relatively limited height in relation to the large footprint of the plot. The treatment of the continuous glass facades is enhanced by the particular attention to detail on the rounded corners, undeniably making light the main quality of this project, compatible with the previous architectural history of Renzo Piano Building Workshop.

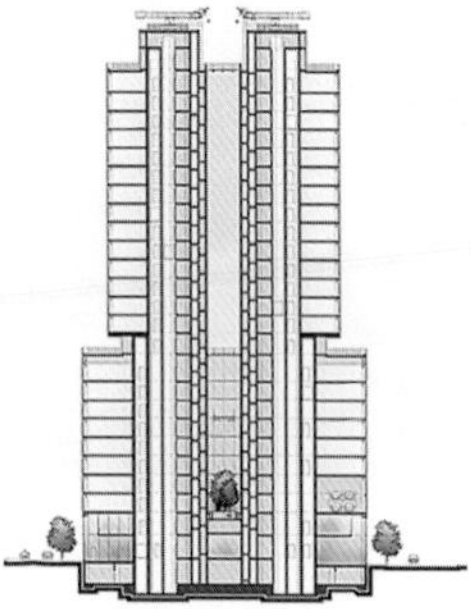

architects
Renzo Piano Building Workshop, SLCE Architects

type
residential

construction
2019

56. 56 Leonard Street

56 Leonard St
New York, NY 10013

external viewing only

+1 212 965 1500

www.56leonardtribeca.com

1 / 2 > Franklin St
A / C / E > Canal St Station

M18 > Church St - Worth St

The project for the residential tower at 56 Leonard Street, designed by the Swiss firm, Herzog & de Meuron, began in 2007 when the developer, Isak Senbahar, purchased the land and air rights from the adjacent New York Law School, a stratagem to ensure a building height that was unequaled in the Tribeca district, and making it the third tallest residential tower in the whole city. The originality of this high-rise design, was the idea to disrupt the classical curtain wall facade common to New York residential towers and office blocks. The architects created a system of cantilevered cell structures, stacking them on top of one another to create unusual irregular facades on all sides of the tower, with constantly changing impact. This aspect is particularly clear on the highest floors where the compact block of the building is interrupted with windows and cantilevered terraces, providing unequaled views and physical contact with the surrounding cityscape.

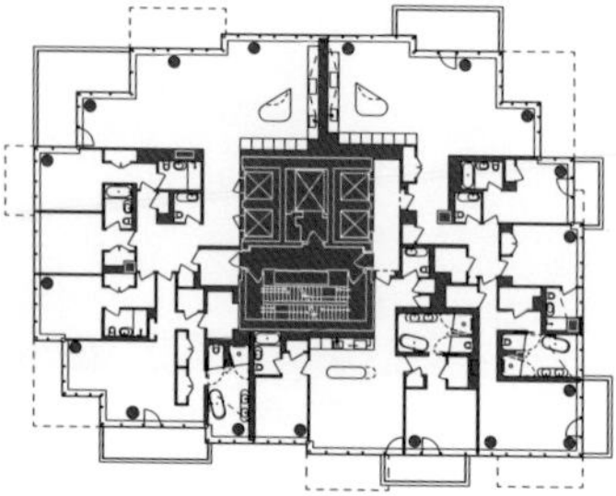

architects
Herzog & de Meuron

type
residential

construction
2016

57. The Woolworth Building

233 Broadway
New York, NY 10007

Mon - Wed - Sat - Sun /
2 pm - 3.30 pm
Tue - Thu / 2 pm - 3 pm
Fri / 1 pm - 3 pm

+1 212 233 2720
info@woolworthbuilding.com
www.woolworthbuilding.com

2 / 3 > Park Place Station
4 / 5 > Fulton St Station
N / R / W > City Hall

The famous Woolworth Building, designed by architect, Cass Gilbert, was built between 1910 and 1913; it is considered one of the most representative skyscrapers constructed in early 20th century America. The building is based on the American Victorian Gothic style, and was one of the first to be built on a steel frame structure. The design is composed of three sections: the base that occupies the whole site area, the shaft, constructed in a U-shape, and finally, the dynamic tower that completes the iconic image of the building. The complicated building structure, 792 feet tall, was made possible because of the collaboration between Gilbert and the structural engineer, Gunvald Aus. In fact, the formal design of the building was strongly influenced by the structural concept, from its foundations, with a complex system of pneumatic form-work, surmounted by a steel beam and grid structure, the wind-bracing elements, and the upper level portal brace arches. The facade, clad in light colored terracotta, in harmony with the characteristic green patina of the copper roof, clearly demonstrates the imposing and distinguished sense of public spirit applied to New York architecture during the period. The building was symbolic of the unwavering modern American spirit, and also the tangible expression of the country's birth as a powerful world economy, which earned the building its title of "Cathedral of Commerce".

architects
Cass Gilbert

type
offices

construction
1913

58. The Fulton Center

200 Broadway
New York, NY 10038

open to the public

+1 212 284 9982
westfieldwtc@westfield.com
www.fultoncenternyc.com

2 / 3 / 4 / 5 >
Fulton St Station

SIM15 > Church St - Fulton St

The building that houses the Fulton Center, subway transit hub and commercial center that can cater to approximately 300,000 passengers per day, was designed by the British firm, Grimshaw in 2014. Without veering from its infrastructural role, this project presents an articulated layout able to control traffic flow towards the lower level subway lines, and acts as a vital link to the Lower Manhattan area; it also provides a space for retail and commercial structures. The five-level building, three above ground and two sub-grade, are constructed around a large atrium roofed by a steel mesh dome that floods the semi-underground transit environment with natural light, expanding and extending the surrounding public space within the structure. The external facade features a series of modular steel columns, recalling the cast-iron pillars in traditional New York architecture. The columns surround the building and act as a support for the vast Sky Reflector-Net dome, that has become a landmark in Lower Manhattan.

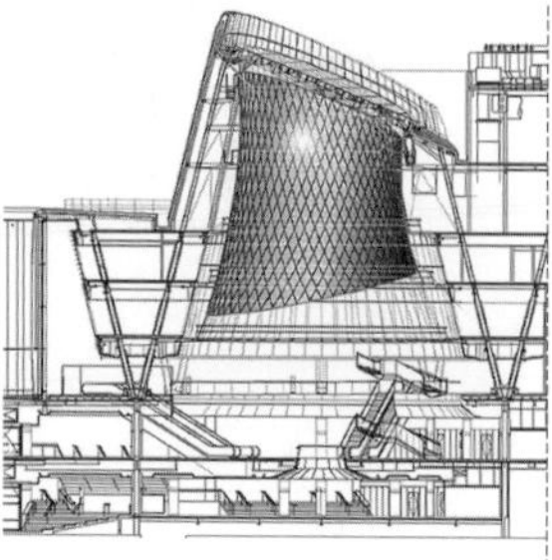

© Grimshaw

architects
Grimshaw

type
retail

construction
2014

59. The Oculus – World Trade Center Transportation Hub

Church St
New York, NY 10006

open to the public

1 > WTC Cortlandt
N / R / W > Cortlandt St Station
4 / 5 > Fulton St Station

M55 > Church St - Liberty St

The imposing transit hub built adjacent to the new World Trade Center designed by Starchitect, Santiago Calatrava, was inaugurated in 2016 after years of problems linked with cost and construction delays. The structure is composed of a monumental system of white steel ribs and glass that form a roof over the vast space below. However, the true impact is revealed in the covered concourse below ground level. The substructural space defined by soaring ribbed elements without any ornamental additions, conveys a strongly symbolic message. This is the great strength of this project: the perception of a structure that is difficult to understand from the exterior, but is revealed in a burst of clarity inside the building. Even in the deeper levels down to subway accesses, this is a space that loses none of its emotional charge, constantly directing the public's gaze upward towards the soaring vertical roof. Finally, this is a powerful symbolic architectural work that declares its ambivalent, artistic rather than architectural value, without denying its intrinsic practical and functional nature. It is the example of how a public building can be transformed into an individualistic personal manifesto.

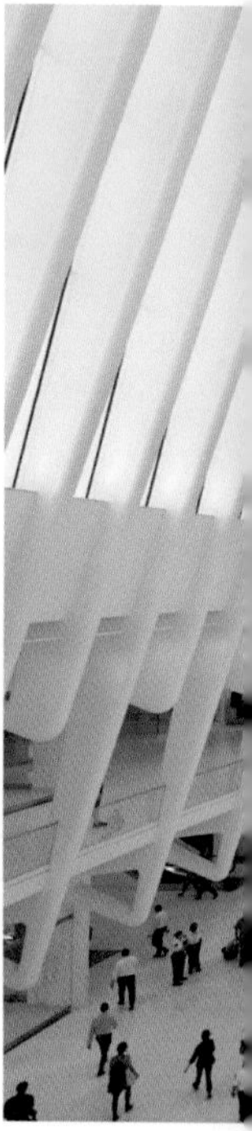

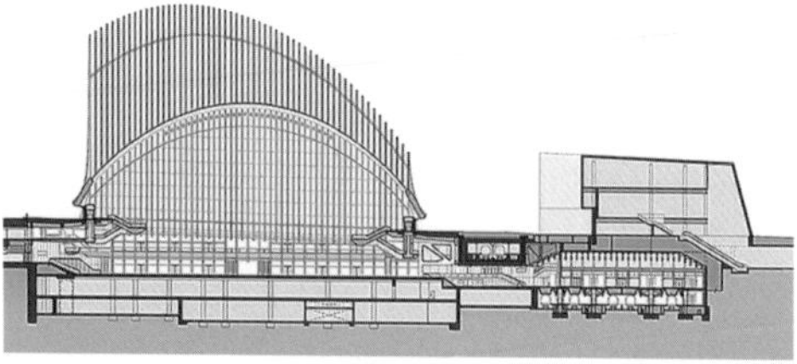

© Santiago Calatrava

architects
Santiago Calatrava

type
subway station

construction
2016

60. Four World Trade Center

150 Greenwich St
New York, NY 10007

Mon - Fri / 9 am - 5 pm

+1 212 490 0666

www.4wtc.com

1 > WTC Cortlandt
N / R / W > Cortlandt St Station
4 / 5 > Fulton St Station

M55 > Church St - Liberty St

The Four World Trade Center Tower, designed by Pritzker Prize winner, Fumihiko Maki, was begun in 2008, as part of a larger reconstruction project for the new World Trade Center. Nearly 980 feet high, the 72-story building assumes the form of a solid vertical element thanks to its exterior skin of floor-to-ceiling ultra-clear glass and extremely geometrical and sharp design. It is destined to become a new landmark on the New York skyline. The base structure of the building, which the architects decided to make open to the public and accessible to the nearby 9/11 Memorial Pavilion, follows the topographic shape of the site, emphasizing the parallelogram form, in line with the first, slimmer building. The last parallelepiped section of the skyscraper shoots up vertically to form the highest part of the building, creating a sequence of pure geometrical volumes that reflect the entire abstract and ever-changing New York cityscape.

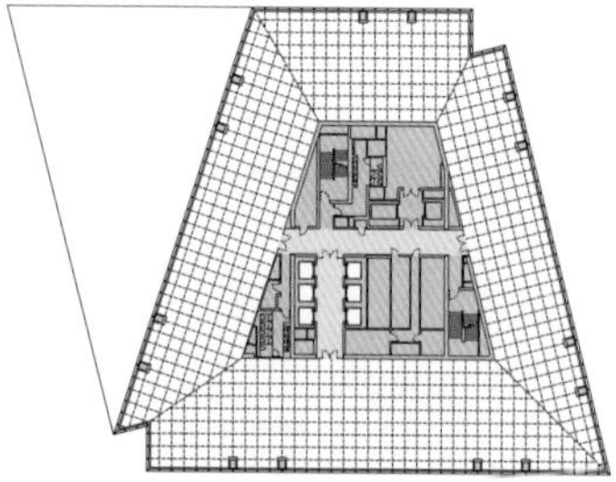

© Joe Woolhead – Courtesy Silverstein Properties

architects
Fumihiko Maki

type
offices

construction
2013

61. 9/11 Memorial Pavilion

180 Greenwich St
New York, NY 10006

open to the public

+1 212 266 5211
reservations@911memorial.
org
www.911memorial.org

1> WTC Cortlandt
N / R / W >
Cortlandt St Station
4 / 5 > Fulton
St Station

M55 > Church St -
Liberty St

The design and construction of a memorial to the tragic events linked with the 9/11 attack was, and still is, a extremely complex project. In this sense, the approach adopted by the international firm, Snøhetta, is based on a concept that is both direct and figurative, close to the late 20th century Deconstructivist tradition, first of all through the volume, that assumes the form of a contemporary archaeological fragment; then the surface of the facade, with the large windows able to display the complex, sometimes chaotic, structural lattice structure in contrast with the alternating opaque and reflective glass surface; lastly, it is in the underground level, rather like a labyrinth, that the true memorial space takes form. This approach focuses on the expression of memory, sometimes even too literally, with all the force and impact of this significant building. In addition, apart from the architectural construction itself, through its semantics, the pavilion plays a sensitive role as a recollection ad perpetuam rei memoriam of an event that is still extremely painful in the collective imaginary, both in New York itself, and throughout the whole country.

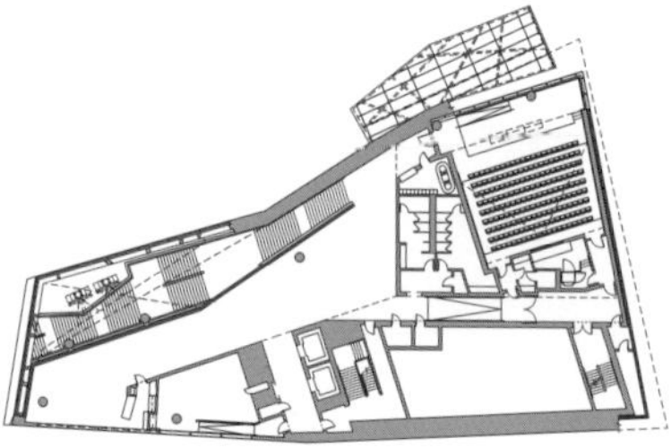

© Snøhetta

architects
Snøhetta

type
memorial

construction
2014

62. National September 11 Memorial

180 Greenwich St
New York, NY 10007

Mon - Sun / 9 am - 8.30 pm

+1 212 312 8800
reservations@911memorial.
org
www.911memorial.org

1 > WTC Cortlandt
N / R / W > Cortlandt St Station
4 / 5 > Fulton St Station

M55 > Church St - Liberty St

The National September 11 Memorial, designed by Michael Arad and landscape designer Peter Walker, was opened in 2011, 10 years after the tragic attack on the Twin Towers. Like the Memorial Pavilion, developed as part of the master plan related to the new World Trade Center, the National September 11 Memorial also had to express the strong and deeply-felt symbolism needed to commemorate the victims of the terrorist attacks. The project design was based on the void as the cardinal theme of the memorial: the footprint of the Twin Tower buildings became the memorial space, with the modification of 'ground zero,' deeply charged with meaning and limited to its most essential form. Two large square reflecting pools, the same size as the footprints and position of the towers, are enclosed by plain black granite parapets, whose slanted surfaces are inscribed with the names of the victims. The pools are 30 feet deep, and channel the water flow towards a central void whose depth is unknown. To complete this somber memorial of sorrow and remembrance, a densely planted wood surrounds the sunken pools as if to protect them, representing an image of a living presence together with the void and absence.

© Handel Architects

architects
Michael Arad, Peter Walker

type
memorial

construction
2011

63. One World Trade Center

285 Fulton St
New York, NY 10007

open to the public

+1 212 257 6600

www.onewtc.com

1 > WTC Cortlandt
N / R / W > Cortlandt St Station
4 / 5 > Fulton St Station

M9 > South End Av - Albany St

The One World Trade Center skyscraper, also known as Freedom Tower, is the most outstanding landmark of the new WTC reconstruction area. Designed by the Skidmore, Owings & Merrill architectural firm, it was built over a period of ten years, and was completed in 2014. Thanks to its antenna, the height of the 104-story, 1776-foot tower symbolizes the year of the Declaration of Independence; with the antenna, it is the tallest building on the American continent, and the sixth highest in the world. The volume of the skyscraper, with its strongly iconic design, is constructed on a blind reinforced concrete square podium base, with the same footprint as the Twin Towers. As the tower rises from the cubic base, its edges are chamfered back, resulting in a faceted form composed of eight elongated isosceles triangles. The resulting geometrical figure, known as antiprism, is highlighted by the materials selected for the composition of the continuous glass facades and underlined by the structural pilaster strips that run up the entire height of the building, increasing the unique vertex effect even further.

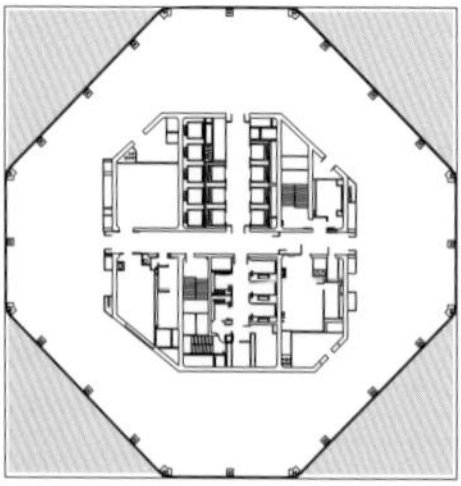

© Skidmore, Owings & Merrill

architects
Skidmore, Owings & Merrill

type
offices

construction
2014

64. Statue of Liberty Museum

1 Liberty Island
New York, NY 10004

open to the public

+1 212 561 4588
ContactUs@ellisisland.org
www.libertyellisfoundation.org

The project for the Statue of Liberty Museum designed by FXCollaborative, was built thanks to a crowd funding campaign that led to the opening of the museum in 2019. It was built to cater to the constant increase in the number of visitors wanting to visit the site, and throughout the museum, ESI Design used interactive media in new and unexpected ways to narrate the Statue's history, and guide the flow of visitors in a fluid efficient manner. The project has an asymmetrical angular layout, and parts of the landscape are raised above the formal arrival mall to create the roof of the museum. The green roof also acts as a panoramic platform with spectacular views of the Statue of Liberty and the New York skyline. The project was designed to create a strong dialogue with Liberty Island and the iconic symbol of the Statue, both charged with great significance, without creating any visual conflict. The museum merges with the landscape to intensify the deeply monumental and symbolic nature of the island.

Battery Park-Liberty Island > Battery Park Terminal

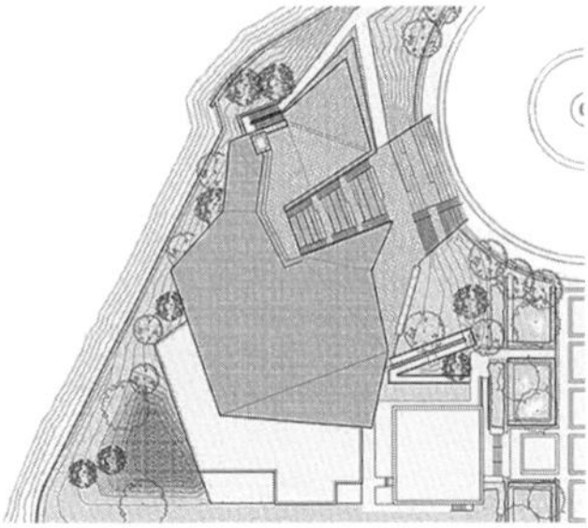

architects
FXCollaborative

type
museum

construction
2019

65. The Hills

Governors Island
New York, NY 11231

Mon - Fri / 10 am - 6 pm
Sat - Sun / 10 am - 7 pm

info@govisland.org
www.govisland.com/the-park

SB (E River Ferry) > Red Hook / Brooklyn Bridge Park Pier 6 → Governors Island

The landscape project for the park on Governors Island, called The Hills, was designed by West 8, and was opened to the public in 2014. Governors Island is located in the New York Harbor, just south of Manhattan. The island covers an area of over 170 acres scattered with medium sized buildings and attracts a steady flow of visitors every year. The project has changed the topographical aspect of the island with hills, pathways and trees to create "conceal and reveal" vistas, and to provide recreational relaxation for visitors. The dense landscape system has developed new panoramas and relaxing areas to create a new park experience. More specifically, the four new hills: Grassy Hill, Discovery Hill, Slide Hill and Outlook Hill, were constructed as a kind of climax in the artificial landscape, enriched by small artistic interventions like the site specific *Cabin* by Rachel Whiteread, integrated into the 2.2 mile promenade winding through the newly planted landscape. The park's physical structure was built using recycled demolition debris, general fill and lightweight pumice, covered by geotechnical reinforcing mesh, rich topsoil, and a carefully selected range of trees and shrubs chosen to prevent sea erosion.

© Timothy Schenck

architects
West 8

type
park

construction
2016

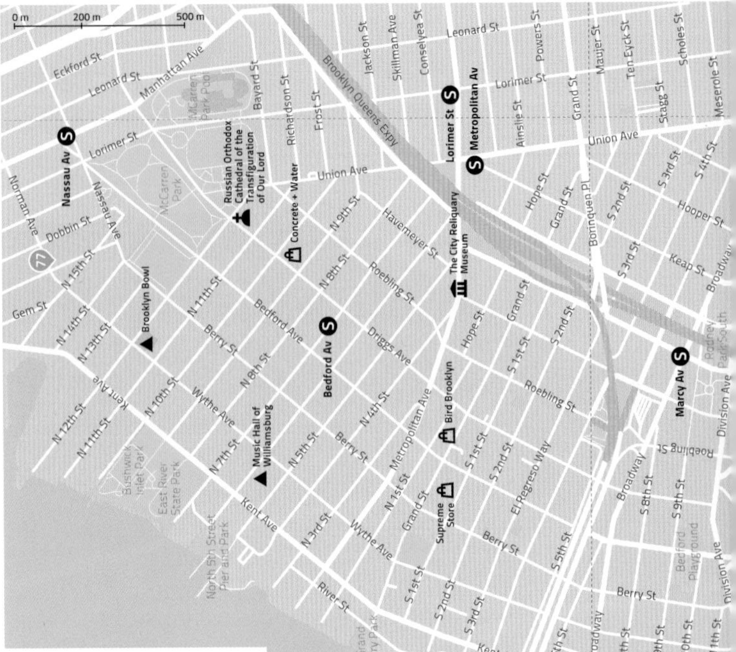

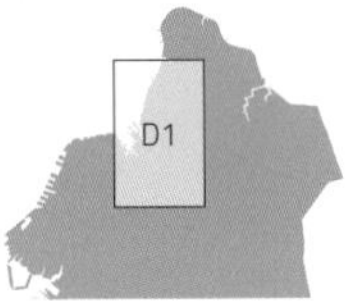

Brooklyn

66. Empire Stores
67. St. Ann's Warehouse
68. Brooklyn Bridge Park
69. Brooklyn Public Library
70. Brooklyn Museum
71. Brooklyn Botanic Garden Visitor Center

Lorimer St
Flushing Av
Myrtle - Willoughby Avs
Bedford - Nostrand Avs
Classon Av
Clinton - Washington Avs
Fulton St
C'mon Everybody
Bar Laika by e-flux
BAM Harvey Theater
Brooklyn Academy of Music
Building 92
Commandant's House
The Brooklyn Hospital Center
Fort Greene Park
Commodore Barry Park
Navy Yard Basin
Taaffe Playground
Classon Playground
Steuben Playground
Underwood Park
Brooklyn Queens Expy
Marcy Ave
Nostrand Ave
Flushing Ave
Park Ave
Myrtle Ave
Willoughby Ave
Dekalb Ave
Lafayette Ave
Greene Ave
Bedford Ave
Franklin Ave
Kent Ave
Classon Ave
Washington Ave
Clinton Ave
Vanderbilt Ave
Carlton Ave
Union Ave
Walworth St
Spencer St
Skillman St
Taaffe Pl
Emerson Pl
Steuben St
Grand Ave
Ryerson St
Hall St
Waverly Ave
Clermont Ave
Adelphi St
Cumberland St
S Oxford St
S Elliott Pl
Washington Park
N Oxford St
N Portland Ave
N Elliott Pl
St Edwards St
Ashland Pl
Rockwell Pl
Welding Rd
Assembly Rd
Paulding St
Market St
14th Ave
Railroad Ave
Gee Ave
Morris Ave
Dock Ave
East Way
West Way
5th St
4th St
3rd St
2nd St
Walton St
Harrison Ave
Gerry St
Middleton St
Heyward St
Lorimer St
Lynch St
Wallabout St
Rutledge St
Hewes St
Lee Ave
Penn St
Hooper St
Keap St
Ross St
Wilson St
Wythe Ave
Stockton St
Vernon Ave
Hart St
Pulaski St
Kosciuszko St
Clifton Pl
Lexington Ave
Quincy St
73
74
75
66
67
68
G
F
E
10
11

Bergen St
Vanderbilt Ave
St Marks Ave
Underhill Ave
Washington Ave
Grand Ave
Dean St
Classon Ave
Pacific
Prospect Pl
Park Pl
Sterling Pl
Butler Pl
St Johns Pl
Plaza St E
Lincoln Pl
N Service Rd
Eastern Pkwy
Park Pl
Eastern Parkway
Brooklyn Museum
Brooklyn Museum
Osborne Garden
Dr. Ronald McNair Park
Botanic Garden
Union St
President St
Brooklyn Botanic Garden
Cranford Rose Garden
Flatbush Ave
Franklin Ave
Carroll St
Crown St
The Donald and Barbara Zucker Natural Exploration Area
69
70
71
12
F
0 m
100 m
250 m

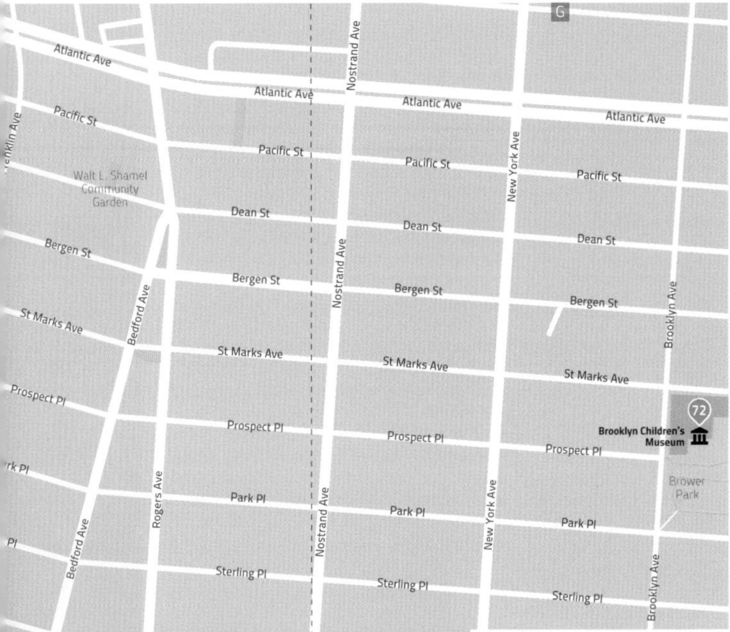

Brooklyn

72. Brooklyn Children's Museum
73. Pratt Institute – Higgins Hall Insertion
74. Building 92
75. New Lab
76. Domino Park
77. A/D/O

66. Empire Stores

53-83 Water St
Brooklyn, NY 11201

open to the public

+1 718 858 8555 /
+1 212 726 0743
dbeare@meqs.com
empirestoresdumbo.com

F > York St Subway Station
A / C > High St - Brooklyn Bridge Station
2 / 3 > Clark St Subway Station

B25 > Front St - York St

ER / SB (E River Ferry) > Wall St - Pier 11 / India St - Greenpoint / South Williamsburg → Dumbo - BBP Pier 1

The Empire Stores renovation project took an abandoned ex-industrial warehouse and transformed it into an enormous center for services and activities for the local community. The New York firm, S9 Architecture, focused on preserving the monumental mass of the building that overlooks the East River. The architects did not alter the external walls, but created openings to provide a pedestrian walk-way through the courtyard to connect the Dumbo urban fabric with the park on the river waterfront. The internal courtyard is defined by glass curtain walls to display the structural layers of the former warehouse.
A system of ramps and stairs leads to the roof which has been transformed into a spectacular panoramic terrace covering an area of about 75,000 square feet. Low profile steel and glass divisions, visible from the exterior, create a connection between the former post-industrial building and the contemporary project.

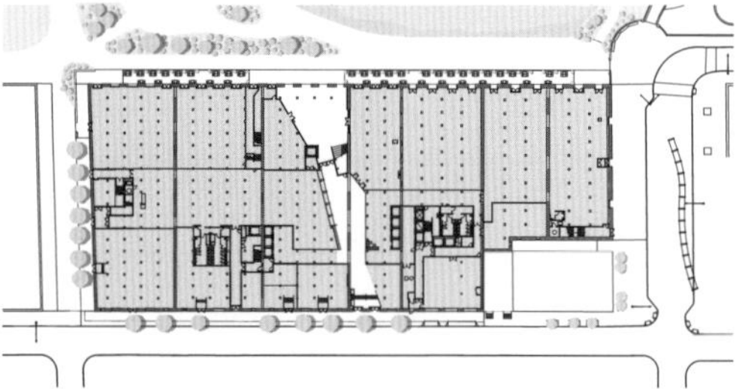

architects
S9 Architecture

type
multi-purpose building

construction
2017

67. St. Ann's Warehouse

45 Water St
Brooklyn, NY 11201

open to the public
by appointment

Mon - Sun / 1 pm - 7 pm

+1 718 254 8779
info@stannswarehouse.org
www.stannswarehouse.org

F > York St Subway Station
A / C > High St - Brooklyn Bridge Station
2 / 3 > Clark St Subway Station

B25 > Front St - York St

ER / SB (E River Ferry) > Wall St - Pier 11 / India St - Greenpoint / South Williamsburg → Dumbo - BBP Pier 1

Tucked beneath the Brooklyn Bridge, is an ex-tobacco warehouse, dating back to 1860; since 2015 it has housed the permanent home of the St. Ann's company, historically one of the most avant-garde, eclectic theatrical companies in USA. The renovation project was designed by the New York firm, Marvel Architects, respecting the building's characteristics. They adopted a delicate but daring solution that permits different configurations, also creating opportunities for merging public and private spaces. The project redefined the original double height structure that frames the city, with a contrast between shade and light, opaque and polished materials placed adjacent to the building's traditional local red brick. A glass and steel volume tops the building around the entire original perimeter to preserve its heritage status.
The interior is divided into three different sections to provide a functional layout for simultaneous but individual uses. A slatted central volume houses the various services and separates the theater from the triangular garden designed by Michael Van Valkenburgh Associates. The theater occupies an open space area with modular seating to accommodate between 300 and 800 people.

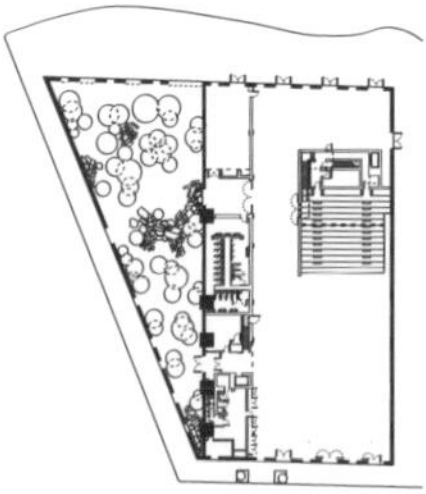

© Marvel Architects

© David Sundberg / ESTO

architects
Marvel Architects

type
theater

construction
2015

68. Brooklyn Bridge Park

334 Furman St
Brooklyn, NY 11201

Mon - Sun / 6 am - 1 am
Pier 2: Mon - Sun /
6 am - 8.30 pm
Pier 5: Mon - Sun /
6 am - 11 pm
Pier 6: Mon - Sun /
8 am - 11 pm

+1 718 222 9939

www.brooklynbridgepark.org

2 / 3 > Clark St Subway Station
A / C > High St - Brooklyn Bridge Station

B61 > Atlantic Ave - Hicks St
B63 > Brooklyn Bridge Pk Rd - Joralemon St

The Brooklyn Bridge Park is the transformation of an abandoned industrial warehouse area into a wonderful urban park. It is part of the vast waterfront redevelopment scheme promoted by the Bloomberg administration aimed not only at improving the quality of the city but also to protect the coastal landscape which is increasingly endangered by flood risk. The project began in 2007, and was spread over five stages to create the extremely strong stone and pile foundations, necessary because of the coastal marshland. This was then protected by a thick belt of planted shrubs.
The park has been designed to fulfill a variety of recreational functions with a diversified landscape that encloses six large piers which had been in disuse since 1983. Each section is aimed at a specific target. For example, Pier 4 is a sandy beach, Pier 5 houses children's playgrounds, sports fields, and a fishing dock. Pier 2 is equipped with sports facilities for basketball, handball, bocce and shuffleboard. Every pier has magnificent views of the Manhattan skyline.

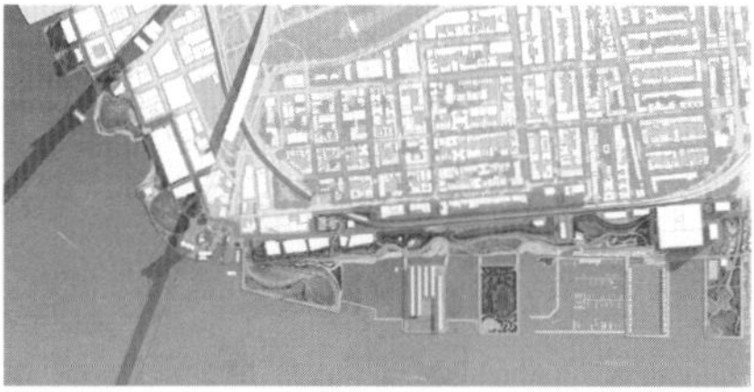

architects
Michael Van Valkenburgh
Associates

type
park

construction
2018

69. Brooklyn Public Library

10 Grand Army Plaza
Brooklyn, NY 11238

Mon - Thu / 9 am - 9 pm
Fri - Sat / 9 am - 6 pm
Sun / 1 pm - 5 pm

+1 718 230 2100

www.bklynlibrary.org

2 / 3 / 4 > Eastern Parkway Brooklyn Museum Station

B41 > Flatbush Ave - Grand Army Plz

The Brooklyn Public Library was founded before Brooklyn was annexed as a part of New York City in 1898. The main library building was designed by Raymond F. Almirall, but only partially completed in the style of early 20th century Beaux Arts style. The final project, which expanded the original design, was partially demolished and in 1941, the library was completely redesigned in Art Déco style.
The library is located on a triangular plot at the northernmost end of Prospect Park, and is divided into three separate blocks. In the center, the curved facade of the main building that houses the entrance, repeats the form of the curved plaza in front of the building. The monumental facade is completely clad in limestone. The tall entrance portal is flanked by two striking pillars decorated with gilded reliefs that celebrate the arts and sciences, combining figures from classical mythology with those of common laborers. The great bronze doors are composed of square frames encasing fifteen iconic figures from American literature, designed by Thomas Hudson Jones, including Tom Sawyer and the whale, Moby Dick.

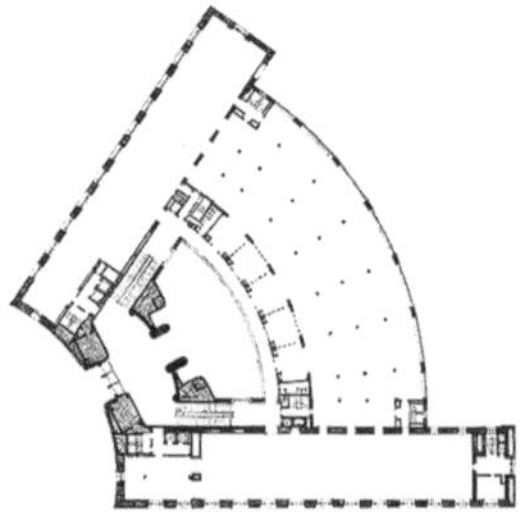

architects
Raymond F. Almirall /
Githens & Keally Architects

type
library

construction
1911 / 1941

70. Brooklyn Museum

200 Eastern Parkway
Brooklyn, NY 11238

Fri - Sun / 11 am - 6 pm
Thu / 11 am - 10 am

+1 718 638 5000
information@
brooklynmuseum.org
www.brooklynmuseum.org

2 / 3 / 4 > Eastern Parkway Brooklyn Museum Station
S > Botanic Garden

B48 > Classon Av - Eastern Parkway

The Brooklyn Museum is one of the oldest and most famous museums in the United States. It is an imposing building designed by the architects, McKim, Mead & White, among the most celebrated exponents of the City Beautiful Movement which developed considerably following the World's Columbian Exposition in 1893. In the same year, the three architects won the competition to design the museum, originally planned to be four times the current size. The opulent facade recalls the classic style of Greek and Roman architecture, enriched with sculptures by important American artists to symbolize all branches of learning. The pediment features the figures of Painting, Sculpture and Architecture.
During the 20th century, the building underwent considerable alterations and renovations. Among the numerous contemporary interventions, in 1990, Arata Isozaki reorganized the internal spaces and partial reconstruction of the museum. In 2004, Ennead Architects designed the large plaza in front of the museum and a semi-spherical entrance pavilion that echoes the original monumental staircase demolished in 1934.

©littleny/iSTOCK / Shutterstock.com

architects
McKim, Mead & White /
Arata Isozaki & Associates /
Ennead Architects

type
museum

construction
1895 / 1990 / 2004

71. Brooklyn Botanic Garden Visitor Center

990 Washington Ave
Brooklyn, NY 11225

Tue - Fri / 8 am - 6 pm, Sat - Sun / 10 am - 6 pm

+1 718 623 7200

www.bbg.org

S > Botanic Garden
2 / 3 / 4 > Nostrand Ave Station

B48 > Classon Ave - President St

Founded in 1910, the Brooklyn Botanic Garden covers a surface of 52 acres with over 12,000 plant species in a widely varied landscape, including a traditional Japanese garden. In 2015, the Weiss/Manfredi firm was commissioned to design an information center and welcome entrance at the ingress in Washington Avenue. The building was designed as a physical and visual threshold to create a barrier between the density of the city and the garden-haven. It was created on an existing embankment to become a true topographical extension of the natural landscape while remaining connected with the long-standing urban surroundings. The fundamental element of the project is a continuous sinuous roof that wanders along the access pathway in a leaf-like shape. The green-roof is covered with a lush garden that blends the architecture with the landscape. It protects the glazed walkways underneath and also acts as a filter and recovery system for rain water run-off. The project incorporates a large number of eco-sustainable functions that run on solar and geothermal power systems.

© Weiss/Manfredi

architects
Weiss/Manfredi

type
museum, info point

construction
2013

72. Brooklyn Children's Museum

145 Brooklyn Ave
Brooklyn, NY 11213

Tue - Fri / 10 am - 6 pm
Sat - Sun / 10 am - 7 pm

+1 718 735 4400

www.brooklynkids.org

2 / 3 / 4 > Nostrand Ave Station
A / C > Kingston - Throop Avs Station

B43 > Kingston Ave - Prospect Pl

The Brooklyn Children's Museum is set in the midst of the densely constructed residential district of Crown Heights, and the expansion project makes a strong impact for its daring design and color. Designed by Rafael Viñoly, the building is clad in yellow ceramic tiles and features porthole windows. The L-shaped layout follows the line of the street and encloses the square core built in 1977. The interior, completely designed to scale for children, houses teaching laboratories, a library, and play areas that stimulate interactive and experiential learning. Even the integrated sustainable energy systems are incorporated into the exhibition spaces, providing an educational experience on the operating function of geothermal wells and integrated energy saving systems.
In 2017, a large pavilion was erected on the panoramic terrace with a canopy structure and flexible furnishings to create multiple spatial configurations.

© Rafael Viñoly Architects

architects
Hardy Holzman Pfieffer /
/ Rafael Viñoly Architects /
Toshiko Mori Architect

type
museum

construction
1977 / 2008 / 2017

73. Pratt Institute – Higgins Hall Insertion

61 St James Pl
Brooklyn, NY 11238

open to the public

+1 718 636 360

www.pratt.edu

G > Classon Ave

B38 > Lafayette Av - Washington Ave

The Brooklyn headquarters of the Pratt Institute house the Architecture faculty. The building was almost completely destroyed by fire and was reconstructed according to a project by Marvel Architects in 2005, including a connecting 'corridor' structure designed by Steven Holl. The layout is based on an H-shape design with the new section inserted between the two historic wings of the complex. The original buildings are linked on each floor with the central hall that compensates the differences in height, highlighting the misalignment of the two facades with a system of red steel horizontal frames. It is interrupted by a series of overlaid square and rectangular elements that mark the east and west entrances. The connecting section features striking contrasts between the translucent and transparent glass planks, enhanced by artificial lighting at night. The double height hall is the main feature of the project; internally it contains a complex system of articulated floors and stairways. Burnt bricks from the fire in the original building have been used to pave the courtyards at the front and rear entrances.

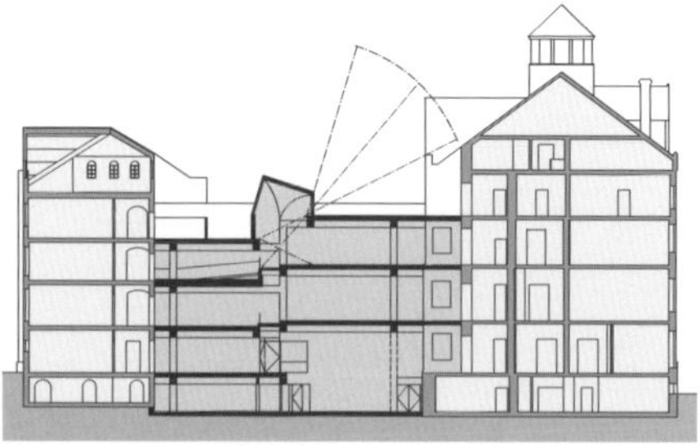

© David Sundberg/ESTO

architects
Steven Holl Architects,
Marvel Architects

type
education

construction
2005

74. Building 92

63 Flushing Ave
Brooklyn, NY 11205

Wed - Sun / 12 am - 6 pm

+1 718 907 5932
info@bnydc.org
www.brooklynnavyyard.org/visit/bldg-92

F > York St Subway Station
A / C > High St - Brooklyn Bridge Station

B57 / B69 > Flushing Ave - Cumberland St

The Brooklyn Navy Yard is a vast industrial naval complex that had been in disuse since 1966, and which is part of a huge urban redevelopment scheme, along with adjacent buildings. Within this area, Building 92 was the previous residence of the Commander of the US Marine Corps, built in 1897, now undergoing renovation and extension work. The original building which was in a bad state of disrepair, had been preserved to maintain its external shell, and to house an exhibition space showing the long manufacturing history of the navy yard.
Behind the northern side, the new building was reconstructed with a steel and glass modular system assembled in only four days, and clad with a steel mesh facade. It houses the administrative offices of various companies and offers a public cafeteria service on the garden-terrace. The internal project integrates sustainable design solutions, which have been certified with international LEED Platinum Status.

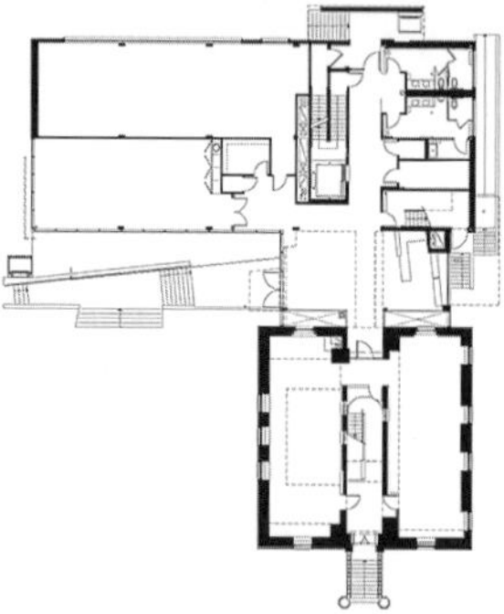

© Beyer Blinder Belle Architects & Planners LLC

© Chuck Choi

architects
Workshop apd,
Beyer Blinder Belle

type
cultural centre

construction
2012

75. New Lab

19 Morris Ave - Building 128
Brooklyn, NY 11205

open to the public
by appointment

+1 718 488 7005

www.newlab.com

F > York St Subway Station
A / C > High St - Brooklyn Bridge Station

B57 / B69 > Flushing Ave - Cumberland St

New Lab is an interesting innovative center for research, development, and manufacturing of new technologies for robotics and artificial intelligence. It occupies a former with 84,000 square feet and the design reflects its industrial factory origins.
The redevelopment project was designed by Marvel Architects who focused on using the vast internal open space to a maximum, creating diversified workstations according to necessity and function. The layout is strongly influenced by the 1889 steel trusswork which supports a series of suspended walkways with connecting staircases. The different sections on the ground floor are created using light, easily assembled partitions to permit different configurations. The original mezzanine level has been converted to provide greater space for open co-working areas. The interior decor was deliberately limited to a black and white palette to act as a background for the brightly colored furnishings, designed and made to measure, among which are certain pieces by Gaetano Pesce and Carlo Mollino.

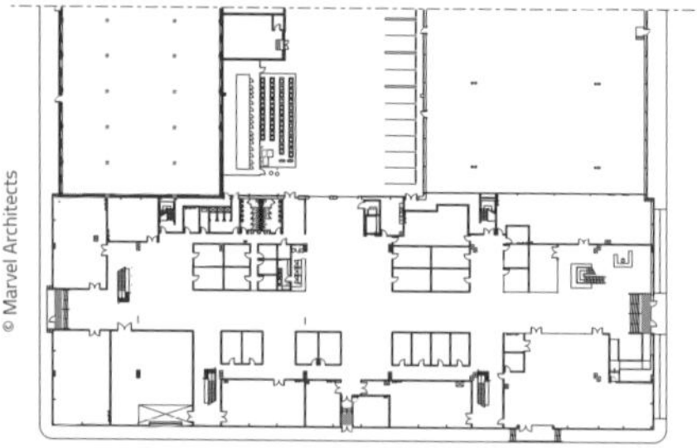

architects
Marvel Architects

type
co-working, research hub

construction
2016

76. Domino Park

300 Kent Ave
Brooklyn, NY 11249

Mon - Sun / 6 am - 1 am

+1 212 484 2700

www.dominopark.com

L > Bedford Ave Station
J / M > Marcy Ave

B32 / Q59 > Kent Ave - 6 St

ER (E River Ferry) > Wall St - Pier 11 / India St - Greenpoint → North Williamsburg

Domino Park is a multi-activity park on the East River waterfront close to the Williamsburg Bridge, at the foot of the former iconic Domino sugar refinery. The master plan, designed by SHoP Architects, divided the area into three functional zones that house a number of cafes, restaurants and recreational facilities destined for the local community. The various zones are connected by a continuous elevated walkway called "artifact walk", along which salvaged ex-refinery equipment has been preserved and integrated as part of the new landscape. The industrial theme children's playground was created by the artist, Mark Reigelman, using materials and elements recovered from the ex-sugar refinery.
Behind the park, the master plan provides for five vast residential and retail complexes, two of which have been completed: 260 Kent designed by COOKFOX Architects and 325 Kent, designed by SHoP Architects.

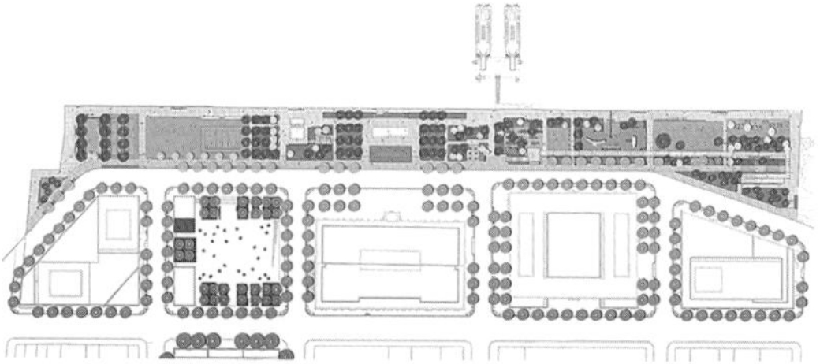

architects
SHoP Architects, James Corner Field Operations

type
park

construction
2018 - ongoing

77. A/D/O

29 Norman Ave
Brooklyn, NY 11222

Mon - Fri / 8 am- 7 pm
Sat: 9 am - 7 pm
Sun: 9 am - 5 pm

sandy@a-d-o.com
www.a-d-o.com

G > Nassau Ave

B46 / B62 >
Manhattan Ave -
Norman Ave

A/D/O is a creative hub financed by MINI to promote new research and startup practices for designers. It occupies a single story building in the Greenpoint district, composed of a rectangular open space (of about 9,800 square feet) that contains a co-working area, studios, work spaces, a design store and a restaurant. The nARCHITECTS reconversion project was aimed at defining a style that reflects the creative role of the center where different functions can merge with each other thanks to a system of reconfigurable modular units. The entrance from Norman Ave features a triangular patio created by removing two brick facades, replaced by two continuous glass curtain walls.
The other street facades were rebuilt using the original building's red bricks, once covered in graffiti, to create a blend of colors; the walls feature large glazed openings. The roof surface was also decorated in bright colors by the artist, Mike Perry, with a striking prism-shaped periscope that emerges from the roof, reflecting the skylines of both Manhattan and Brooklyn.

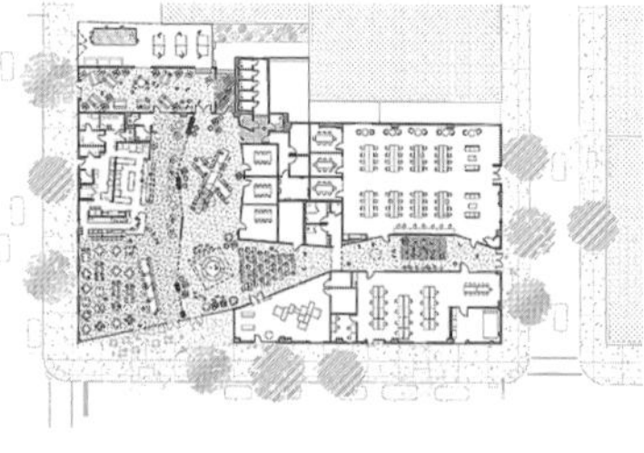

© Frank Ouderman

architects
nARCHITECTS

type
co-working, research hub

construction
2017

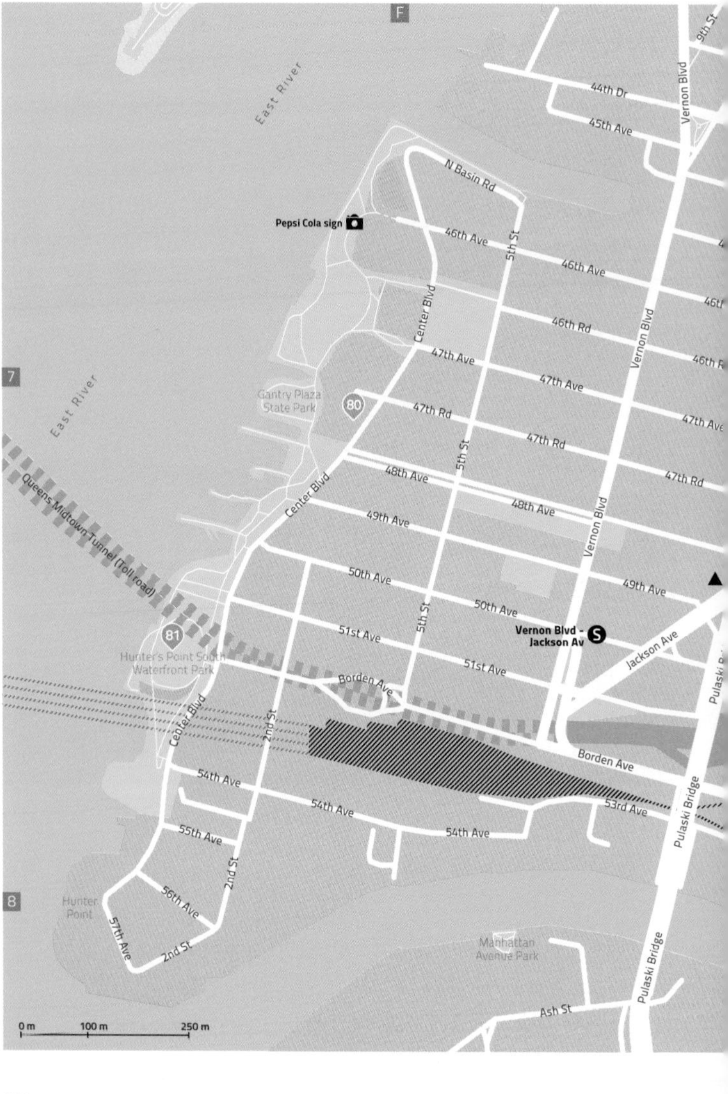

F
7
8
East River
East River
44th Dr
45th Ave
Vernon Blvd
9th St
N Basin Rd
Pepsi Cola sign
46th Ave
5th St
46th Ave
Center Blvd
46th Rd
Vernon Blvd
47th Ave
47th Ave
Gantry Plaza State Park
80
47th Rd
47th Rd
5th St
48th Ave
Center Blvd
48th Ave
49th Ave
Vernon Blvd
Queens Midtown Tunnel (Toll road)
50th Ave
49th Ave
50th Ave
5th St
81
51st Ave
Vernon Blvd - Jackson Av
Jackson Ave
Hunter's Point South Waterfront Park
51st Ave
Borden Ave
Center Blvd
2nd St
Borden Ave
54th Ave
54th Ave
53rd Ave
54th Ave
55th Ave
Pulaski Bridge
2nd St
56th Ave
Hunter Point
57th Ave
2nd St
Manhattan Avenue Park
Pulaski Bridge
Ash St
0 m
100 m
250 m

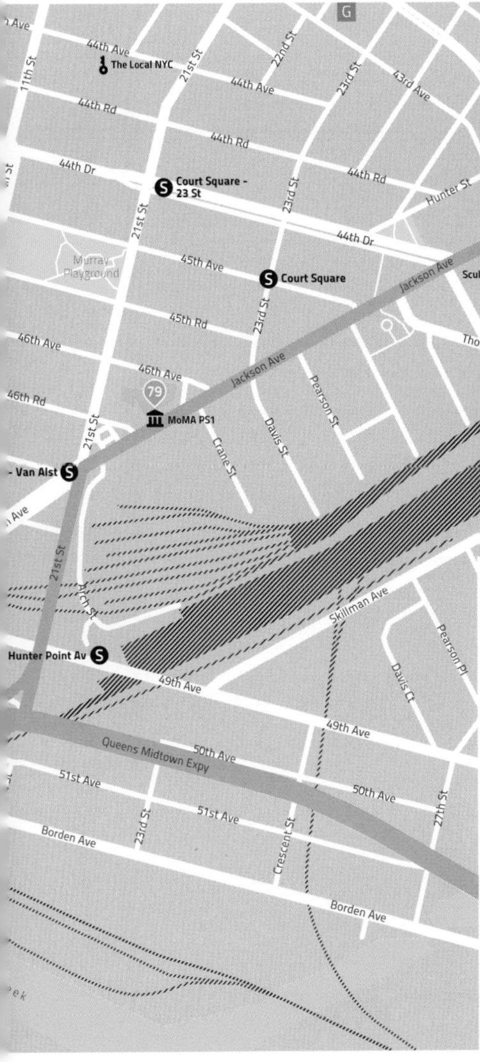

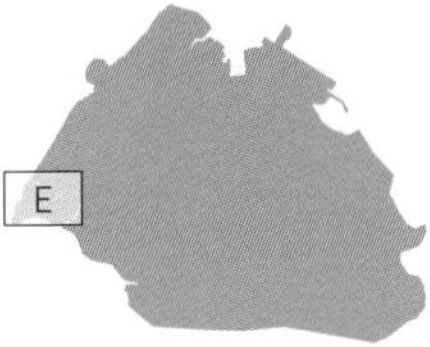

Queens

78. SculptureCenter
79. MoMA PS1
80. Hunters Point Community Library
81. Hunter's Point South Waterfront Park
82. The Noguchi Museum
83. Flushing Meadows Corona Park
84. New York State Pavilion

78. SculptureCenter

44-19 Purves St
Long Island City, NY 11101

Thu - Mon / 11 am - 6 pm

+1 718 361 1750
info@sculpture-center.org
www.sculpture-center.org

E / R > Queens Plaza Subway Station
7 > Court Square

B62 > Jackson Ave - 43 Ave
Q67 > Jackson Ave - Dutch Kills St

Since 2002, the SculptureCenter has been housed in a post-industrial brick building in Purves Street, Long Island City. It was founded in 1928 under the name of The Cay Club, and was the pioneering center for promoting experimental art in New York. The building, a former trolley repair shop from 1908, was redesigned by Chinese-American artist and designer Maya Lin, followed by a renovation and expansion in 2014 by Andrew Berman Architect. The project has significantly improved the exhibition space quality and usability, and has provided an additional new building adjacent to the original center to contain the entrance lobby and bookstore. The new addition follows the same existing rectangular layout, and is connected to the original gallery by a small glazed corridor, with a large patio at the end. The interior of the main building is surprisingly spacious, light and airy, accentuated by the strong steel truss structure. The original facade was maintained unchanged, except for the windows, and the adjacent low facade is clad with Corten steel panels.

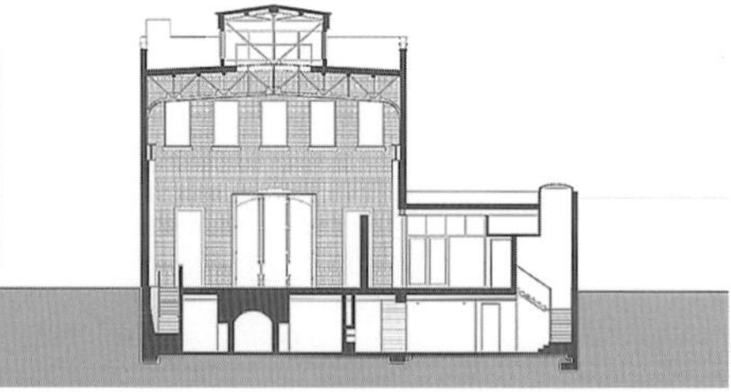

© Andrew Berman Architect

© Andrew Berman Architect

architects
Maya Lin Studio / Andrew Berman Architect (restoration, extension)

type
museum

construction
2002 / 2014

79. MoMA PS1

22-25 Jackson Ave
Long Island City, NY 11101

Thu - Mon / 12 am - 6 pm

+1 718 784 2084
info@moma.org
www.momaps1.org

7 > Court Square
G > 21 St - Van Alst Station

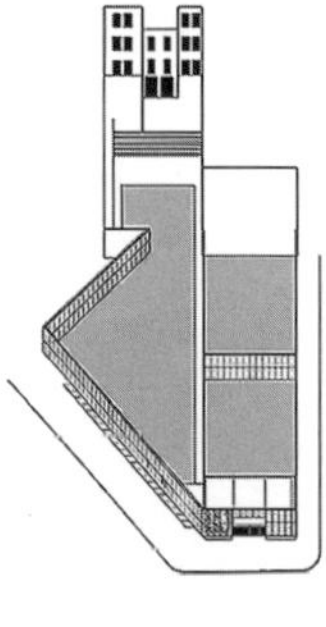

© Andrew Berman Architect

MoMA PS1 is a nonprofit institution that promotes experimental contemporary art, and was founded through the affiliation of MoMA with the Art Center set up in the 1970s.
The building that houses the Center was built in 1892 as the first public school in Long Island City. The PS1 Contemporary Art Center opened its first major exhibition in 1976, and the building reopened in 1997 after a building-wide renovation. In 2011, the New York architect Andrew Berman designed a new entrance building to be used for entry, ticketing, orientation and art display. The new project was adapted to the geometry of the plot and the materiality of the site, with roof, wall and floor surfaces all in exposed concrete. The uniformity of the concrete, contrasting only with the window frames, is interrupted by wall slots and transversal clerestory openings that create a dynamic effect, filtering natural light into the interior space. In 2014 Andrew Berman Architect then renovated four floors of galleries within the south wing of the complex, providing museum grade climate control and humidification, allowing an expansion in the range of shows and art that can be shown.
Among the numerous and innovative activities promoted by the Center, every year, The Young Architects Program (YAP) transforms the large internal courtyard with site-specific installations. This competition has helped launch renowned architects like Andrés Jaque and Jenny Sabin.

© Andrew Berman Architect

architects
Andrew Berman Architect

type
museum

construction
2011, 2014 (extension)

80. Hunters Point Community Library

47 Center Blvd
Long Island City, NY 11101

open to the public

www.queenslibrary.org

7 > Vernon Blvd - Jackson Ave

Q103 > Vernon Blvd - 47 Rd

ER > E 34th St / India St - Greenpoint → Hunters Point South

The district of Hunters Point in Long Island City is undergoing vast urban development aimed at increasing the quality of public services in Queens. Among the numerous projects, Steven Holl Architects has designed a public library, which was opened in 2019, following a long construction period.
The building can be clearly seen from Manhattan as it is located almost opposite the United Nations Headquarters. It is a sculptural block of painted exposed concrete, with large glazed geometrical openings in the facade to reveal the internal stairways flanked by book shelving. The main east facade features sculpted cutouts that show the articulated interior layout divided into three thematic sections for children, adolescents and adults. A roof-garden offers spectacular panoramic views of the city. The library is also surrounded by a planted wood of ginkgo trees enclosed to the east by an outdoor reading area and a low office building.

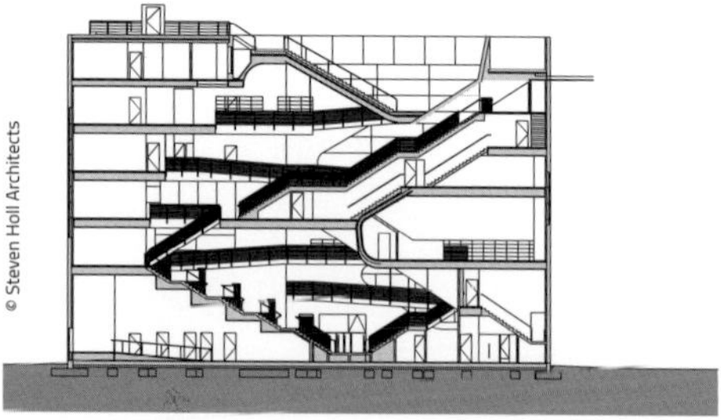

architects
Steven Holl Architects

type
library

construction
2019

81. Hunter's Point South Waterfront Park

Center Blvd
Long Island City, NY 11101

Mon - Sun / 6 am - 10 pm

+1 212 639 9675
info@hunterspointparks.org
www.hunterspointparks.org

7 > Vernon Blvd - Jackson Ave

Q103 > Vernon Blvd - Borden Ave

ER (E River Ferry) > E 34th St / India St - Greenpoint → Hunters Point South

Hunter's Point South Waterfront Park is the vast scheme for the redevelopment of a post-industrial site covering 30 acres on the southern side of the East River. It is an extremely diversified design that includes landscaping, architecture, infrastructures and art in a single project, providing the public with a blend of recreational and cultural activities. The result of a multidisciplinary collaboration between two New York firms, the park is considered a model of urban ecology that incorporates innovative sustainable design solutions.
It is separated from the urban fabric by a thick belt of shrubs planted to follow the natural contours of the site and reestablish the marshland along the river. The main access to the park is marked by a narrow pedestrian bridge that connects the lower part of the park, including cycling paths, with a cantilevered, 30-foot tall viewing platform, facing the Manhattan skyline. On the opposite side is a pavilion for recreational activities that features a continuous protective awning system that incorporates solar panels and a rain water recycling system.

architects
SWA/Balsley, Weiss/Manfredi

type
park

construction
2018

82. The Noguchi Museum

9-01 33rd Road
Long Island City, NY 11106

Wed - Fri / 10 am - 5 pm,
Sat - Sun / 11 am - 6 pm

+1 781 204 7088

www.noguchi.org

N / V > Broadway

Q103 / Q104 >
Vernon Blvd - 33 Rd

Founded in 1985, The Noguchi Museum was designed and created by the Japanese-American sculptor, artist, and designer Isamu Noguchi and is located in the Long Island City studio that he designed with architect Shoji Sadao. It was an important first step in the metamorphosis of a Queens neighborhood that has developed into a flourishing cultural and artistic hub. The complex was expanded by incorporating an adjacent 1920s building in typical Queens red brick industrial style with large openings. In 2016, the New York firm Sage and Coombe Architects completed a three-phase, publicly-funded project to rethink and renovate the space. The Museum is an extremely evocative space accessed through a large garden that links Oriental tradition with Noguchi's personal spatial concept; perhaps the maximum expression of this concept was his *Garden of Peace*, created in Paris in 1958. The permanent collection was curated and installed by the artist; it flows into the garden and continues though the ground floor of the galleries. The other spaces host temporary exhibitions. Another section houses vast historical archives, and a renowned center for international research, which also offers scholarships for emerging artists.

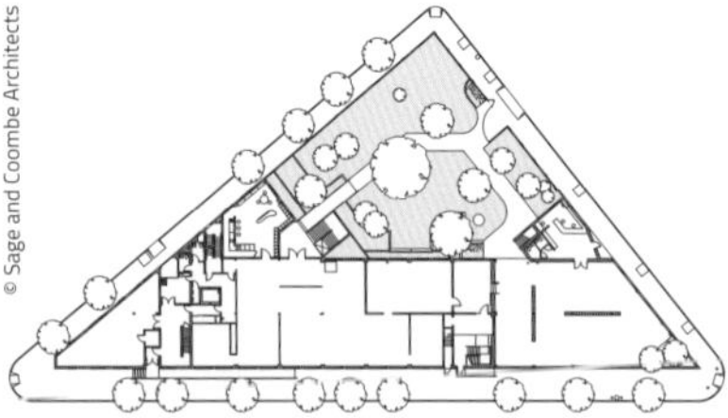

architects
Isamu Noguchi, Shoji Sadao /
Sage and Coombe Architects

type
museum

construction
1985 / 2016

83. Flushing Meadows Corona Park

111st St
Queens, New York

open to the public

+1 718 760 6565

7 > 111st St

Q23 > 102 St - 34 Ave

Flushing Meadows Corona Park is the fourth largest public park in the city covering an area of 897 acres. It was originally used as a dumping ground for construction waste, and was described as "a valley of ashes" in Francis Scott Fitzgerald's novel, *The Great Gatsby*. It was Robert Moses who promoted the huge plan to reclaim the site for parkland. It later hosted the New York World's Fair in 1939, a pioneering event to celebrate the achievement of international industrial design. The park was used again for the 1964 World's Fair, but preserved part of the existing layout in Beaux-Arts architectural style. The *Unisphere*, theme symbol of the 1964 Expo, forms the central core that connects the routes leading to the four sectors of the park. The whole area features a diversified landscape with a wide variety of botanical species. The park includes shopping malls, recreational areas, extensive sports facilities and open green spaces. Among the buildings that were preserved, the Queens Museum, built in 1939, houses a comprehensive section about the history of the park and the American Expo.

architects
Gilmore David Clarke /
Michael Rapuano

type
park

construction
1939 / 1964

84. New York State Pavilion

Flushing Meadows Corona Park
Queens, New York

open to the public

+1 718 760 6565

7 > 111st St / Mets - Willets Point

Q23 > 102 St - 34 Ave

The New York State Pavilion is a little-known project by Philip Johnson designed for the 1964 New York World's Fair in the Central Section of the park. With its distinctive space-age aesthetics, the project was part of the Googie architectural trend that was prevalent between the forties and the sixties, and which played a fundamental role, not only in architecture and design, but as an influence on American culture in general. Johnson's design plan was to define a free space with no particular function; an architectural design able to represent New York without relying on traditional exhibitions or staging. The Pavilion was initially built as a temporary structure, but was then preserved, although today, it is no longer used and is in a state of decay.
The Pavilion is composed of three different structures. The main structure, Tent of Tomorrow, is elliptical in plan, and was covered by a steel frame based on a bicycle spokes system. To one side, three tall observatory towers, resembling flying saucers, provided vast views of the park as far as Manhattan. The small theater is still in use, although the design has been altered considerably following restoration and extension work.

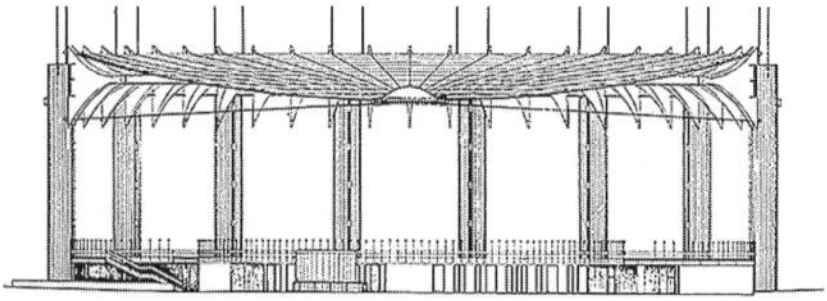

architects
Philip Johnson / Alfredo De Vido / Caples Jefferson Architects

type
multipurpose space

construction
1964 / 1993 / 2009

Museums

Cooper Hewitt Smithsonian Design Museum
Museum dedicated to international design
-
2 E 91st St, New York, NY 10128

www.cooperhewitt.org
chtours2@si.edu
Tel +1 212 849 8351

El Museo del Barrio
Museum of Latin American art
-
1230 5th Ave, New York, NY 10029

www.elmuseo.org
Tel +1 212 831 7272

Frick Collection
Private collection
-
1 East 70th St, New York, NY 10021

www.frick.org
info@frick.org
Tel +1 212 288 0700

Hans Hollein Feigen Gallery
contemporary art gallery
-
27 E 79th St, New York, NY 10075

www.rlfeigen.com
info@rlfeigen.com
Tel +1 212 628 0700

Italian American Museum
Museum of Italian-American art
-
155 Mulberry St, New York, NY 10013

www.italianamericanmuseum.org
info@ItalianAmericanMuseum.org
Tel +1 212 965 9000

Leo Castelli Gallery
Gallery of contemporary art
-
18 E 77th St, New York, NY 10075

www.castelligallery.com
info@castelligallery.com
Tel +1 212 249 4470

National Museum of the American Indian
Museum of American Indian art
-
1 Bowling Green, New York, NY 10004

www.americanindian.si.edu
nmai-ny-education@si.edu
Tel +1 212 514 3705

Neue Galerie
Museum of early 20th century German and Austrian art and design
-
1048 5th Ave, New York, NY 10028

www.neuegalerie.org
visitorservices@neuegalerie.org
Tel +1 212 628 6200

New York Transit Museum
Museum dedicated to public transportation
-
99 Schermerhorn St, Brooklyn, NY 11201

www.nytransitmuseum.org
Tel +1 718 694 1600

Soho Contemporary Art
American contemporary art gallery
-
259 Bowery, New York, NY 10002

www.sohocontemporaryart.com
info@sohocontemporaryart.com
Tel +1 646 719 1316

Storefront for Art and Architecture
Architecture, art and design gallery
-
97 Kenmare St, New York, NY 10012

www.storefrontnews.org
info@storefrontnews.org
Tel. +1 212 431 5795

Tenement Museum
Immigration museum
-
103 Orchard St, New York, NY 10002

www.tenement.org
Tel. +1 877 975 3786

The Broken Kilometer
Indoor installation by Walter De Maria
-
393 W Broadway, New York, NY 10012

Tel + 1 212 925 9397

The Drawing Center
Art gallery of historical and contemporary drawings
-
35 Wooster St, New York, NY 10013

www.drawingcenter.org
info@drawingcenter.org
Tel +1 212 219 2166

The Earth Room
Indoor installation by Walter De Maria
-
141 Wooster St, New York, NY 10012

Tel +1 212 989 5566

The Skyscraper Museum
Skyscraper history and design museum
-
9 Battery Pl, New York, NY 10280

www.skyscraper.org
info@skyscraper.org
Tel +1 212 945 6324

Theaters

Apollo Theater
253 W 125th St, New York, NY 10027

www.apollotheater.org
info@apollotheater.com
Tel +1 212 531 5300

Circle in the Square Theatre
1633 Broadway, New York, NY 10019

www.circlesquare.org
info@circlesquare.org
Tel +1 212 307 0388

David H. Koch Theater
20 Lincoln Center Plaza, New York, NY 10023

www.davidhkochtheater.com
customercare@davidhkochtheater.com
Tel +1 212 496 0600

Gershwin Theater
222 W 51st St, New York, NY 10019

www.gershwin-theater.com
support@gershwin-theater.com
Tel +1 212 586 6510

New World Stages
340 W 50th St, New York, NY 10019
www.newworldstages.com/
Info@NewWorldStages.com
Tel +1 212 239 6200

Shubert Theater
225 W 44th St, New York, NY 10036
www.shubert.nyc
tickets@telecharge.com
Tel +1 212 239 6210

St. James Theatre
246 W 44th St, New York, NY 10036
www.jujamcyn.com
jujamcyn@jujamcyn.com
Tel +1 800 653 8000

The Broadway Theater
1681 Broadway, New York, NY 10019
www.broadway.com
ticketing@broadway.com
Tel +1 212 239 6200

United Palace
4140 Broadway, New York, NY 10033
www.unitedpalace.org
info@unitedpalace.org
Tel +1 212 568 6700

Restaurants

• • • expensive
• • mid-range
• inexpensive

Atrium DUMBO
• •
15 Main St, Brooklyn, NY 11201
www.atriumdumbo.com
info@atriumdumbo.com
Tel +1 718 858 1095

Bar Laika by e-flux
• •
224 Greene Ave, Brooklyn, NY 11238
www.laika.bar
enquire@efluxbarlaika
Tel + 1 347 529 4321

Chef's Table at Brooklyn Fare
• • •
431 W 37th St, New York, NY 10018
www.brooklynfare.com
Tel +1 718 243 0050

Chelsea Market
•
75 9th Ave, New York, NY 10011
www.chelseamarket.com
Tel +1 212 652 2111

Dean & DeLuca
•
1150 Madison Ave, New York, NY 10028
www.deandeluca.com
Tel +1 212 717 0800

Last Light Cocktail Bar
• •
225 Bowery, New York, NY 10002
www.lastlight.nyc
enquire@lastlight.nyc
Tel +1 646 343 4500

Nathan's Famous
•
1205 Riegelmann Boardwalk, Brooklyn, NY 11224
www.nathansfamous.com
Tel +1 718 975 1905

Shake Shack
•
Madison Square Park, New York, NY 10010
www.shakeshack.com

Uncle Jack's Steakhouse
••
440 Ninth Avenue, New York, NY 10001
www.unclejacks.com
Tel +1 212 244 0005

Hotels

••• expensive
•• mid-range
• inexpensive

Best Western Convention Center Hotel
•••
522 W 38th St, New York, NY 10018
www.bestwestern.com
Tel +1 212 405 1700

Chelsea Savoy Hotel
••
204 W 23rd Street, New York, NY 10011
www.chelseasavoynyc.com
info@chelseasavoynyc.com
Tel +1 212 929 9353

HI New York City Hostel
•
891 Amsterdam Ave, New York, NY 10025
www.hiusa.org
NewYork@hiusa.org
Tel +1 212 932 2300

Morningside Inn
••
235 W 107th St, New York, NY 10025
www.morningsideinn-ny.com
info@morningsideinn-ny.com
Tel +1 212 316 0055

Soho Grand Hotel
••
310 W Broadway, New York, NY 10013
www.sohogrand.com
info@sohogrand.com
Tel +1 212 965 3000

The Local NYC
•
1302 44th Ave, Long Island City, NY 1110
www.thelocalny.com
info@thelocalny.com
Tel +1 347 738 5251

The Ritz-Carlton
•••
50 Central Park, New York, NY 10019
www.ritzcarlton.com
cpguest@ritzcarlton.com
Tel +1 212 308 9100

The Roxy Hotel
••
2 6th Ave, New York, NY 10013
www.roxyhotelnyc.com
guestrelations@roxyhoteltribeca.com
Tel +1 212 519 6600

The Tillary Hotel Brooklyn
••
85 Flatbush Ave Ext, Brooklyn, NY 11201
www.thetillaryhotel.com
Tel + 1 718 329 9537

Stores

Apple Fifth Avenue - electronics store
767 5th Ave, New York, NY 10153
www.apple.com
Tel +1 212 336 1440

Assouline - bookstore
68 5th Ave, New York, NY 10019
www.assouline.com
Tel +1 212 593 7236

Beacon's Closet - clothing store
10 W 13th St, New York, NY 10011
www.beaconscloset.com
Tel +1 917 261 4863

Bird Brooklyn - clothing store
203 Grand St, Brooklyn, NY 11211
www.birdbrooklyn.com
Tel +1 718 388 1655

Bloomingdale's - clothing store
1000 3rd Ave 59th St, New York, NY 10022
www.bloomingdales.com
Tel +1 212 705 2000

Casa Magazines - bookstore
22 8th Ave, New York, NY 10014
Tel + 1 212 645 1197

FAO Schwarz - toy store
30 Rockefeller Plaza, New York, NY 10111
www.faoschwarz.com
Tel +1 800 326 8638

Macy's - clothing store
422 Fulton St, Brooklyn, NY 11201
www.macys.com
Tel +1 718 875 7200

Manolo Blahnik - clothing store
31 W 54th St, New York, NY 10019
www.manoloblahnik.com
Tel +1 212 582 3007

Mast Books - bookstore
72 Ave, New York, NY 10009
www.mastbooks.com
Tel +1 646 370 1114

Matter Store - design
405 Broome St, New York, NY
www.mattermatters.com
Tel +1 212 343 2600

MoMA design store - bookstore / design store
81 Spring St, New York, NY 10012
www.store.moma.org
Tel +1 646 613 1367

Nepenthes New York - clothing store
307 W 38th St, New York, NY
www.nepenthesny.com
Tel +1 212 643 9540

R & Company - design store
82 Franklin St, 64 White St, New York, NY 10013
www.r-and-company.com
Tel + 1 212 343 7979

Strand Bookstore - bookstore
828 Broadway 12th St, New York, NY 10003
www.strandbooks.com
Tel +1 112 473 1452

Supreme Store - clothing store
152 Grand St, Brooklyn, NY 11249
www.supremenewyork.com
Tel +1 718 599 2700

Tiffany & Co. - jewellery / accessories
727 5th Ave, New York, NY 10153
www.tiffany.it
Tel +1 212 755 8000

Young Designers Market - design store
268 Mulberry St, New York, NY 10013
www.youngdesignersmarket.com
Tel +1 073 844 2440

Architectual offices

Andrew Berman Architect
77 Chambers St, New York, NY 10007
www.andrewbermanarchitect.com
info@andrewbermanarchitect.com
Tel +1 212 226 5998

Beyer Blinder Belle
120 Broadway, New York, NY 10271
www.beyerblinderbelle.com/
info@bbbarch.com
Tel + 1 212 777 7800

Bjarke Ingels Group
45 Main St, Brooklyn, NY 11201
www.big.dk
nyc@big.dk
Tel +1 347 549 4141

Caples Jefferson Architects
37-18 Northern Boulevard,
Long Island City, NY 11101
www.capjeff.com
office@capjeff.com
Tel +1 212 779 9772

CetraRuddy
1 Battery Plaza, New York, NY 10004
www.cetraruddy.com
info@cetraruddy.com
Tel +1 212 941 9801

Cooper Robertson
123 William St, New York, NY 10038
www.cooperrobertson.com
info@cooperrobertson.com
Tel +1 212 247 1717

Diller Scofidio + Renfro
601 W 26th St, New York, NY 10001
www.dsrny.com
info@dsrny.com
Tel +1 212 260 7971

Ennead Architects
320 W 13th St, New York, NY 10014
www.ennead.com
info@ennead.com
Tel +1 212 807 7171

ESI Design
111 5th Ave Floor 12, New York, NY 10003
www.esidesign.com
Tel +1 212 989 3993

Foster + Partners
300 W 57th St, New York, NY 10019
www.fosterandpartners.com
webshot@fosterandpartners.com
Tel +1 212 641 9600

FXCollaborative
22 W 19th St, New York, NY 10011
www.fxcollaborative.com
info@fxcollaborative.com
Tel +1 212 627 1700

Grimshaw Architects
637 W 27th St, New York, NY 10001
www.grimshaw.global
Tel +1 646 293 3600

Handel Architects
120 Broadway, New York, NY 10271
www.handelarchitects.com
NewYork@handelarchitects.com
Tel + 1 212 595 4112

Herzog & de Meuron
199 Lafayette St, New York, NY 10012
www.herzogdemeuron.com
info@herzogdemeuron.com
Tel +1 212 966 8460

James Corner Field Operations
475 10th Ave, New York, NY 10018
www.fieldoperations.net
info@fieldoperations.net
Tel +1 212 433 1450

Marvel Architects
145 Hudson St, New York, NY 10013
www.marvelarchitects.com
press@marvelarchitects.com
Tel +1 212 616 0420

Maya Lin Studio
112 Prince St, New York, NY 10012
www.mayalin.com
Tel +1 646 590 0046

Michael Van Valkenburgh Associates
16 Court Street, Brooklyn, NY 11241
www.mvvainc.com
mvva_ny@mvvainc.com
Tel +1 718 243 2044

Morphosis
153 W 27th St, New York, NY 10001
www.morphosis.com
studio@morphosis.net
Tel +1 424 258 6200

Morris Adjmi Architects
60 Broad St 32nd Flr, New York, NY 10004
www.ma.com/
info@ma.com
Tel +1 212 982 2020

nARCHITECTS
68 Jay St, Brooklyn, NY 11201
www.narchitects.com
press@nARCHITECTS.com
Tel +1 718 260 0845

OMA
180 Varick St, New York, NY 10014
www.oma.eu
ny-office@oma.com
Tel +1 212 337 0770

Pei Cobb Freed & Partners
88 Pine St, New York, NY 10005
www.pcf-p.com
pcf@pcf-p.com
Tel +1 212 751 3122

Pelli Clarke Pelli Architects
322 8th Ave, New York, NY 10001
www.pcparch.com
InfoNYC@pcparch.com
Tel +1 212 417 9496

Populous
475 5th Ave, New York, NY 10017
www.populous.com
Tel +1 917 261 3426

Rafael Viñoly Architects
50 Vandam St, New York, NY 10013
www.vinoly.com
Tel +1 212 924 5060

Renzo Piano Building Workshop
827 Washington St, New York, NY 10014
www.rpbw.com
newyork@rpbw.com
Tel +1 212 400 2302

S9 Architecture
460 W 34th St, New York, NY 10001
www.s9architecture.com
office@s9architecture.com
Tel +1 212 457 4077

Sage and Coombe Architects
12 Vestry St, New York, NY 10013
www.sageandcoombe.com
office@sageandcoombe.com
Tel +1 212 226 9600

Santiago Calatrava
713 Park Ave, New York, NY 10021
www.calatrava.com
Tel +1 212 452 1046

Selldorf Architects
860 Broadway, New York, NY 10003
www.selldorf.com
info@selldorf.com
Tel +1 929 352 8131

SHoP Architects
233 Broadway, New York, NY 10279
www.shoparc.com
studio@shoparc.com
Tel +1 212 889 9005

Snøhetta
80 Pine St, New York, NY 10005
www.snohetta.com
contact@snohetta.com
Tel +1 646 383 4762

SOM
14 Wall St 25th, New York, NY 10005
www.som.com
Tel +1 212 298 9300

Steven Holl Architects
450 W 31st St, New York, NY 10001
www.stevenholl.com
mail@stevenholl.com
Tel +1 212 629 7262

Studio Gang
50 Broad St, New York, NY 10004
www.studiogang.com
press@studiogang.com
Tel +1 212 579 1514

Thomas Balsley Associates
31 W 27th St, New York, NY 10001
www.swabalsley.com
contact@swabalsley.com
Tel +1 212 684 9230

Toshiko Mori Architect
199 Lafayette St, New York, NY 10012
www.tmarch.com
info@tmarch.com
Tel +1 212 337 9644

Weiss/Manfredi
200 Hudson St, New York, NY 10013
www.weissmanfredi.com
info@weissmanfredi.com
Tel +1 212 760 9002

West 8
333 Hudson St, New York, NY 10013
www.west8.com/ny
Tel +1 212 285 0088

Workshop apd
39 W 38th Street, New York,
NY 10018
www.workshopapd.com
info@workshopapd.com
Tel +1 212 273 9712

Index by architect

Index by project

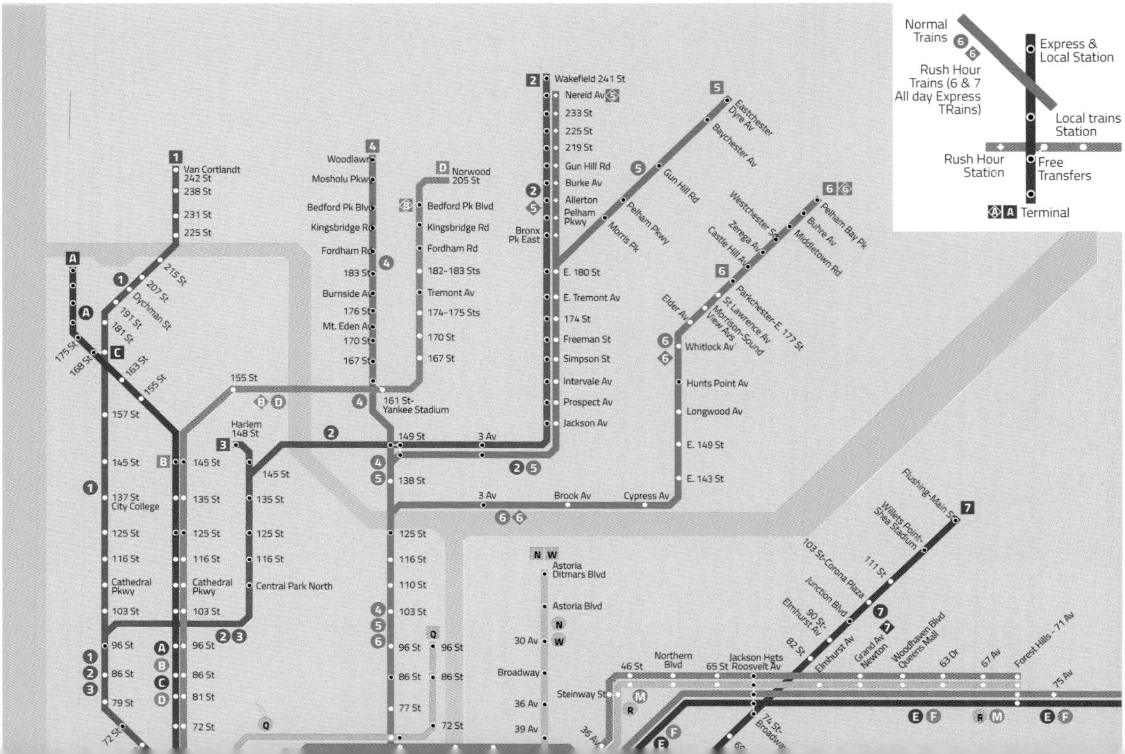

Normal Trains
Rush Hour Trains (6 & 7 All day Express TRains)
Express & Local Station
Local trains Station
Rush Hour Station
Free Transfers
Terminal
Van Cortlandt 242 St
238 St
231 St
225 St
215 St
207 St
Dychman St
191 St
181 St
175 St
168 St
163 St
155 St
157 St
145 St
137 St City College
125 St
116 St
Cathedral Pkwy
103 St
96 St
86 St
79 St
72 St
81 St
Harlem 148 St
135 St
Central Park North
Woodlawn
Mosholu Pkwy
Bedford Pk Blvd
Kingsbridge Rd
Fordham Rd
183 St
Burnside Av
176 St
Mt. Eden Av
170 St
167 St
Norwood 205 St
182-183 Sts
Tremont Av
174-175 Sts
161 St-Yankee Stadium
149 St
3 Av
138 St
110 St
77 St
Wakefield 241 St
Nereid Av
233 St
219 St
Gun Hill Rd
Burke Av
Allerton
Pelham Pkwy
Bronx Pk East
E. 180 St
E. Tremont Av
174 St
Freeman St
Simpson St
Intervale Av
Prospect Av
Jackson Av
Eastchester Dyre Av
Baychester Av
Morris Pk
Pelham Bay Pk
Buhre Av
Middletown Rd
Westchester Sq
Zerega Av
Castle Hill Av
Parkchester-E. 177 St
St Lawrence Av
Morrison-Sound View Avs
Elder Av
Whitlock Av
Hunts Point Av
Longwood Av
E. 149 St
E. 143 St
Cypress Av
Brook Av
Astoria Ditmars Blvd
Astoria Blvd
30 Av
Broadway
36 Av
39 Av
Steinway St
46 St
Northern Blvd
65 St
Jackson Hgts Roosevelt Av
74 St-Broadway
Flushing-Main St
Willets Point-Shea Stadium
111 St
103 St-Corona Plaza
Junction Blvd
90 St-Elmhurst Av
82 St
Elmhurst Av
Grand Av Newton
Woodhaven Blvd Queens Mall
63 Dr
67 Av
Forest Hills - 71 Av
75 Av

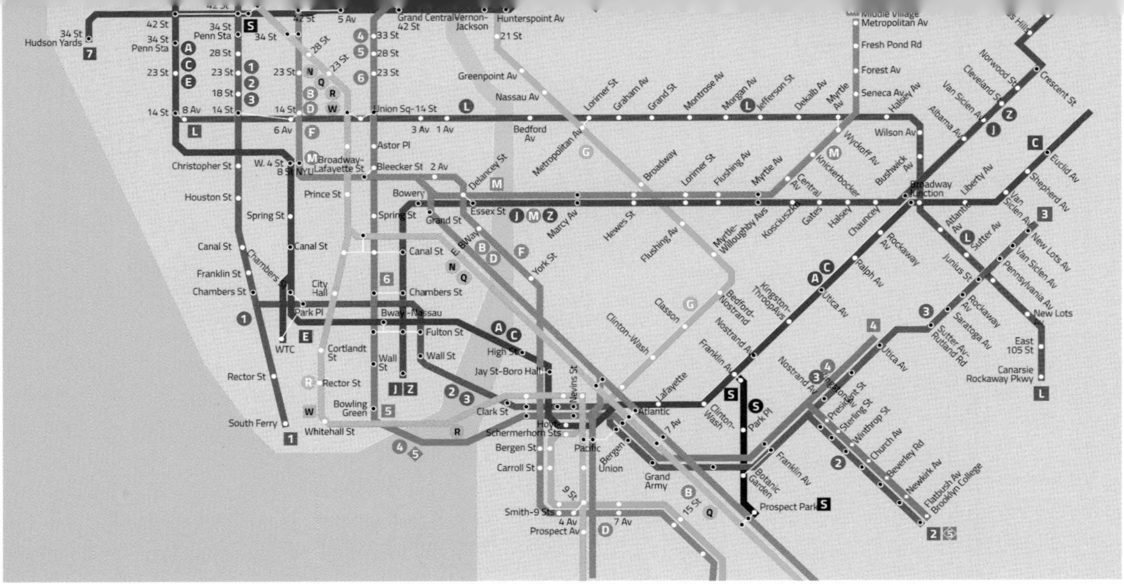

1 242 St, Bronx / South Ferry, Manhattan

2 241 St, Bronx / Flatbush Av, Brooklyn

3 148 St, Manhattan / New Losts Av, Brooklyn

4 Woodlaw, Bronx / Utica Av, Brooklyn

5 238 St or Dyre Av, Bronx / Bowling Green or Flatbush Av

6 Pelham Bay Park or E. 177 St, Bronx / Brooklyn Bridge, Manhattan

7 Main St, Queens / 34 St - Hudson Yards, Manhattan

7 Main St, Queens / 34 St - Hudson Tards, Manhattan

S Times Square, Manhattan / Grand Central, Manhattan

S Franklin Av, Brooklyn / Prospect Park, Brooklyn

A 207 St, Manhattan / Lefferts Blvd or the Rockaways

C 168 St, Manhattan / Euclid Ave, Brooklyn

E Jamaica Center, Queens / WTC - Chambers St, Manhattan

S Broad Channel, Queens / Rockaway Park, Queens

B Bedford Pk Blvd or 145 St / Brighton Beach, Brooklyn

D 205 St, Bronx / Coney Island, Brooklyn

F 179 St, Queens / Coney Island, Brooklyn

G Court Sq, Queens / Church Av, Brooklyn

L 8 Av, Manhattan / Rockaway Pkwy, Brooklyn

J Jamaica Center, Queens / Broad St, Manhattan

M Metropolitan Av, Queens / 71 - Continetal Avs, Queens or Essex St

Z Jamaica Center, Queens / Broad St, Manhattan

N Ditmars Blvd, Queens / Coney Island, Brooklyn

R 71 - Continental Avs, Queens / 95 St, Brooklyn

Q 96 St, Manhattan / Coney Island, Brooklyn

W Ditmars Bvld, Queens / Whitehall St, Manhattan

Photolithography
LAB di Gallotti Giuseppe Fulvio, Florence

This volume was printed in November 2019
by Gutenberg Press Limited, Gudja Road, Tarxien,
Malta PLA 19